DESTINATION COFFEE

60 Recipes from Around the World

›—‹

COFFEE RECIPES AND PHOTOGRAPHY BY THERESA DUNCAN

To every coffee farmer who nurtures a four-year process from seed to plant to bean.
To every barista who pours a bit of happiness in every cup.
To my dear family and friends who encouraged my coffee adventures.

Published by Tirona Publishing

Copyright © 2024 by Theresa Duncan

All rights reserved.

No portion of this book may be reproduced in any form without written permission from the author, except as permitted by U.S. copyright law. If you would like permission to use material from this book, please contact DestinationCoffee60@gmail.com. Thank you for your support of the author's rights.

https://www.instagram.com/goodeats_coffeeandsweets/

Book design by Christine Foltzer
Editing by Claire Atkinson
Coffee Styling and Photography by Theresa Duncan

ISBN 979-8-9896118-1-2

10 9 8 7 6 5 4 3 2 1

First edition 2024

TABLE OF CONTENTS

INTRODUCTION 10
    Saving Wildlife through Eco-friendly Coffee Production 14

COFFEE FUNDAMENTALS AND METHODS 20
    Brewing Equipment 20
    Espresso Machine 22
    Coffee Beans 23
    Milk Options 25
    How to Steam and Froth Milk 26
    Coffee Mugs, Cups, and Glasses 28
    Homemade Whipped Cream 28

COFFEE RECIPES 31
    Affogato in Florence 32
    Airplane Coffee 35
    Arabic Coffee in Abu Dhabi 36
    Bulletproof Coffee in Silicon Valley .. 39
    Caffè Americano in the USA 40
    Café Au Lait in Paris 43
    Café con Miel in Valencia 44
    Café Cubano in Havana 47
    Café de Olla in Mexico City 48
    Cafe Hafuch in Tel Aviv 51
    Café Mocha in Mokha 52
    Cappuccino in Milan 55
    Charcoal Coffee in Cairo 56
    Chicory Café Au Lait in New Orleans ... 59
    Coconut Milk Coffee in Kona 60
    Coffee and Cola Float in Rio de Janeiro 63
    Coffee Jelly in Batangas 64
    Coffee Lassi in Mumbai 67
    Coffee Liqueur in Veracruz 68
    Cold Brew in Tokyo 71
    Cortado in Basque Country 72
    Dalgona Coffee in Seoul 75
    Eggnog Latte in London 76
    Einspänner in Vienna 79
    Es Alpukat in Jakarta 80
    Espresso in Milan 83
    Espresso Martini in Sydney 84
    Espresso Romano, Origin Unknown 87
    Flat White in Melbourne and Wellington 88
    Frappe in Athens 91
    Gingerbread Latte in the North Pole ... 92
    Glariffee in Sonoma 94
    Horchata Cold Brew in Lagos 98
    Iced Blended Oreo™ Coffee in Los Angeles 100
    Iced Coffee in Kyoto 103
    Irish Coffee in Shannon 104
    Jamaican Coffee in Kingston 107

Kaffeost in Northern Scandinavia 108

Kaisermelange in Vienna 110

Kopi Jahe in Medan 113

Latte in Reykjavik 114

Maple Whipped Cream Coffee in Quebec City . . 117

Mazagran in Mazagran 118

Mocha Frappuccino in Boston 121

Mocha Latte Hot Chocolate Bomb in Boise 122

Moroccan Coffee in Marrakesh 127

Oliang in Bangkok 128

Peppermint Mocha Latte in the North Pole 131

Pour Over Coffee in Stratford-upon-Avon 132

Pumpkin Spice Latte in Seattle 135

Raktajino on Planet Kronos 136

Rice Coffee in the Western Visayas 139

Ristretto, Espresso, and Lungo in Rome 140

Sea Salted Iced Coffee in Taipei 143

S'mores Latte in Everytown, USA 144

Strong Coffee Fika in Stockholm 146

Tinto in Bogotá 149

Turkish Coffee in Istanbul and Tbilisi 150

Vietnamese Iced Coffee in Hanoi 153

White Russian in Moscow 154

World's Best Cup of Coffee in New York City . . . 156

Yuanyang in Hong Kong 159

ACKNOWLEDGMENTS 160

INDEX 162

CITATIONS 164

INTRODUCTION

It's that one moment when I feel like I've finally arrived in a new place. I'm sipping coffee in a café, in a country I'm visiting for the very first time. An outdoor café in Paris just steps away from Notre-Dame. A cozy interior looking out over the city of Tbilisi. A coffeehouse with a thatched roof of palm fronds on the island of Bohol.

I like to look for the coffee preparation found only in that place, the most local choice I can find on the menu, or I seek out the guidance of the local barista. I settle into my café seat and take in my surroundings. I make a note of the table details—the single stem of a rosebud in Nantes, the modern vase that contrasts with the antiquity of Athens' Parthenon in the distance, the candlelight at breakfast on a winter's morning in Reykjavik.

I close my guidebook and set aside my map. In this moment, I am focused on the lovely cup of coffee before me. I gently lift the cup in my hands. I can't help but close my eyes ever so briefly as I take in the familiar scent of coffee. I savor my first sip, reveling in the comfort of coffee. Then I dive into the discovery. What taste is this? A smoky scent in San Miguel de Allende. A rich chocolate undertone in Baguio. A gelato melting in espresso in Rome.

In March 2020, I found myself cut off from all travel as the entire world grappled with the realities of the Covid-19 pandemic. The entire world paused with grave concern about a disease that we were just beginning to understand. We worried for the health and safety of ourselves, our loved ones, and our communities. We witnessed the suffering of those who were seriously ill and the courage of our frontline workers.

As the economy closed to all but essential services, we saw millions stressed with the burden of financial hardship. We lost loved ones and we often grieved alone, unable to gather together as the pandemic continued to spread.

As we began to understand the severity of coronavirus, it became clear that life would not soon be returning to normal. In just a few short weeks, most of the world entered some level of lockdown and travel was all but eliminated. Like everyone else, I was worried and stressed. I took every precaution to care for others by staying home to avoid spreading the virus.

I wasn't sure how to navigate this new reality, but I knew I needed to focus on something positive. And, I needed to find a way to satiate my wanderlust. I've always loved coffee, especially when traveling to new places. I had an idea: I thought I would attempt to make a few coffees

from around the world as a way to stay connected to my love of travel, even if I couldn't leave my home. And that is where this journey begins.

What began as making a few coffees to pass the time soon became a fulfilling and exciting adventure. I found myself daydreaming of coffee recipes and researching coffee traditions. Instead of making travel itineraries, I started making ingredient lists. Instead of buying airplane tickets, I started ordering saffron, panela, and vanilla beans. Instead of researching museums, I experimented with several varieties of steamed milk.

I thought I'd make half a dozen coffees, but I couldn't stop. I was having too much fun! It was a welcome break from the endless pandemic worries, and it kept me joyfully connected to the world. We may have been alone during the quarantine, but we all live on this beautiful blue marble together, as Carl Sagan once famously noted. By studying the history of coffee traditions and culture, I was reminded of how connected we all are, the same reminder that is presented to us, over and over again, as we travel to new countries.

As I started this journey, the only coffee skill I had was pushing a button on a Kcurig coffee maker. Now, 60 recipes later, a whole new world has opened up for me, all from the comfort of my own kitchen.

Most of all, I'm hoping you'll enjoy this adventure with me. Because what is better than a cup of coffee in a new city? A second cup to share with a new friend. Enjoy!

SAVING WILDLIFE THROUGH ECO-FRIENDLY COFFEE PRODUCTION

An essay by Wildlife Conservation Society Colombia and Fundación Grupo Argos[1]

EVERY TIME YOU PURCHASE COFFEE, YOU'RE MAKING A DECISION THAT CAN HELP OR HARM WILDLIFE.

Just as most of us prefer to purchase recycled paper to reduce deforestation, we also have a choice when it comes to our beloved coffee beans. What many consumers don't yet know is that the way in which coffee beans are grown and produced has a direct impact on the survival of some of the world's most endangered wildlife.

To illustrate the connection between wildlife and coffee beans, let's explore an inspiring case study in South America. The Andean bear

(*Tremarctos ornatus*) is the only bear species in South America and the last living species of short-faced bears in the world. The species is distributed along the Andean tropical region encompassing Venezuela, Colombia, Ecuador, Perú, Bolivia, and northern Argentina.

Andean bears are often referred to as spectacled bears for their distinctive white rings that make it appear as if they are wearing eyeglasses. Light-colored markings are also found on their head, throat, and chest and are unique to each individual. Growing up to 5 to 6 feet long, Andean bears can weigh up to 350 pounds. They climb trees and build platforms made of sticks to reach and forage for food at higher elevations.

Andean bears also fulfill an important role within the ecosystem as a seed disperser. Although the Andean bear is classified as a carnivore, the species mainly consumes plants and fruits, and after consumption, the bear's stomach acids activate the germination processes of the seeds. As the germinated seeds are expelled, the bear helps disperse more than 200 plant species from their diverse diet across the highlands of the Tropical Andes.

THROUGHOUT THE REGION, ANDEAN BEARS ARE THREATENED BY HUMAN ACTIVITIES SUCH AS HABITAT ENCROACHMENT, ILLEGAL HUNTING, CATTLE RANCHING, AGRICULTURE, AND CLIMATE CHANGE.

Andean bears live in tropical forests adjacent to, and often within, coffee bean farms. This close proximity to rural communities has put humans and wildlife in conflict. With a decrease in habitat and natural food sources, Andean bears have resorted to raiding crops and attacking domestic cattle. As a result of this conflict and other threats, Andean bears are listed by the International Union for Conservation of Nature (IUCN) Red List of Threatened Species as Vulnerable.

IN COLOMBIA, WE'RE WORKING ON A SOLUTION.

In 2015, a public-private partnership led by National Natural Park system of Colombia, Fundación Grupo Argos, Corporación Auntónoma Regional del Valle del Cauca, Fundación Smurfit Kappa Colombia, and Wildlife Conservation Society was established to conserve Andean bears in Colombia. The main goal of this program, Conservamos la Vida (We

Preserve Life), is to maintain viable populations of Andean bears in five core areas across Colombia. A viable population is defined as having at least 50 active reproductive individuals across a landscape, which requires a minimum of 3,800 km² of natural habitat.

To achieve this goal, the Conservamos la Vida program offers support to communities to help develop wildlife-friendly coffee farming and production practices. Using the best science available, the program provides farmers with the training and tools to reuse wastewater from coffee as organic fertilizer, improve coffee infrastructure at each farm, and improve the collection of coffee beans to enhance the quality of the product.

"CAFÉ OSO ANDINO" ANDEAN BEAR COFFEE

The Colombian town of El Águila is located in the foothills of the Western Cordillera in the buffer zone adjacent to the Tatamá National Natural Park—a park known for its rich biodiversity of endemic and near-endemic species. This fertile region is known for its importance for Andean bear conservation and its production of high-quality coffee.

The Conservamos la Vida program signed a total of 16 conservation agreements with farmers in this locality to maintain 481 hectares of natural habitat for Andean bears and improve 170 hectares of productive areas within the farms. Over time, this dynamic collaboration with farmers led to the creation of a formal association of coffee producers committed to Andean bear conservation. Thus, a new brand of coffee was launched.

The *Café Oso Andino* (Andean Bear Coffee) is a high-quality coffee produced using sustainable practices with low environmental impacts. *Café Oso Andino's* coffee profile is described as:

> *Black chocolate, fruitty, and caramelized aroma with a taste of black sugar cane, melao, chocolate notes, light spices, medium acidity, and pleasant residual. Finally, a balanced body.*

After six years of working with the El Águila community, the association is now well-known for producing a high-quality coffee with cupping profiles between 82-86 (on a 100 point scale, this high score indicates a high quality of coffee). At the time of printing, *Café Oso Andino* is successfully being exported to the United States and the United Arab Emirates, and will soon be certified with the Andean bear-friendly label, which will yield higher margins and profits to the local farmers and open up access to organic and wildlife-friendly international markets.

At the beginning of the program, coffee producers reported a low presence of wildlife within their farms. Today, the coffee producers and Andean bear protectors are happy to report a significant increase in bear sightings in their farms as well as increased numbers of white-tailed deer, cougars, tayras, oncillas, and 25 other mammal species as a result of their wildlife-friendly productive activities.

Thanks to the dedicated work of coffee farmers in El Águila town along with support from Conservamos la Vida program, the future of Andean bears in Colombia is improving. Communities have learned that they can coexist with wildlife and that Andean bear conservation provides a new, more profitable and sustainable model for coffee producers to improve their livelihoods.

COFFEE FOR WILDLIFE

Café Oso Andino is just one of many new success stories that demonstrate how nature-friendly coffee production can both protect wildlife and bring more profits to local growers. Making informed decisions can be challenging, but there are good resources available. As you consider your coffee bean purchases, research the origin and ethics of your favorite coffee brands, ask your local coffeeshop questions about how they source

their beans, and seek out coffee farmers that align with your interests and values as a consumer. With your help, we can save the Andean bear and many other vital species.

ESSAY CO-AUTHORED BY:

Mauricio Vela-Vargas, Wildlife Conservation Society Colombia, Bogotá, Colombia PhD
Luisa Rincon-Bustamante, Wildlife Conservation Society Colombia, Bogotá, Colombia
Maria Camila Villegas, Fundación Grupo Argos. Medellin, Colombia
Theresa Duncan, Wildlife Conservation Society, Global Resources, California, MBA
Germán Forero-Medina, Wildlife Conservation Society Colombia, Bogotá, Colombia

WILDLIFE CONSERVATION SOCIETY (WCS)

WCS combines the power of its zoos and an aquarium in New York City and a Global Conservation Program in more than 50 countries to achieve its mission to save wildlife and wild places. WCS runs the world's largest conservation field program, protecting more than 50 percent of Earth's known biodiversity; in partnership with governments, Indigenous People, Local Communities, and the private sector. It's four zoos and aquarium (the Bronx Zoo, Central Park Zoo, Queens Zoo, Prospect Park Zoo, and the New York Aquarium) welcome more than 3.5 million visitors each year, inspiring generations to care for nature.

COFFEE FUNDAMENTALS AND METHODS

Within this book, you will find a wide variety of coffee recipes—from the simple to the complex. As we journey around the world, we will explore a diverse set of superlatives, such as the most traditional coffee, the most famous, the most inventive, or the most obscure. This is not a comprehensive inventory of coffee recipes and traditions, but rather an assortment of recipes designed to delight and surprise coffee novices and aficionados, alike.

Brewing Equipment

Your preferred brewing device

Throughout this cookbook, many recipes call for a brewed cup of coffee. In these recipes, you can use any of the methods illustrated on the right. While I prefer the flavor of coffee made in a French press, I use all of the following devices and you can, too! No matter your current preference, I invite you to try out these different methods. Each one produces a slightly different taste and sensory experience. The reason I love a pour-over is the intimacy of the brew—there is no machine as an interface. It's simply you, coffee, glass, a simple filter, and water. You may be surprised by which one creates the best experience for you!

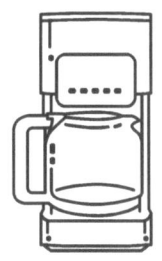

AUTOMATIC OR MANUAL
DRIP COFFEE MAKER
(MOST COMMON)

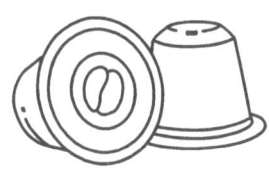

CAPSULE COFFEE MAKERS
(SUCH AS A KEURIG OR
NESPRESSO)

POUR-OVER
(SUCH AS A CHEMEX)

FRENCH PRESS

AREOPRESS

COLD BREW

STOVETOP MAKER
(SUCH AS A MOKA POT)

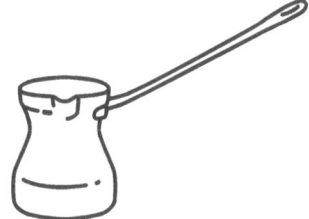

TURKISH COFFEE MAKER
(IBRIK)

STOVETOP POT
(STILL A COMMON METHOD
IN MANY PLACES)

Espresso Machine

If you're new to making espresso, please do not be intimidated—it's much easier than you might think. You can start your journey with an automatic or semi-automatic espresso machine. You can make an excellent espresso at home and I promise it will revolutionize your at-home coffee experience. Trust me.

For the seasoned barista, you've likely already graduated to the manual espresso machine and you have the art of pulling a shot down to a science.

There are many variations and options available, but the most common espresso machines fall into the following three categories:

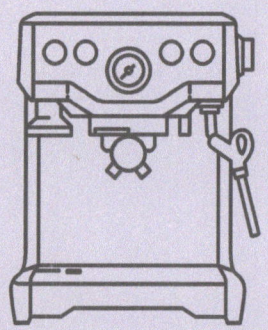

AUTOMATIC ESPRESSO MACHINE

This is ideal for the beginner, yet it will create an outstanding shot of espresso. You'll add the water and the espresso grounds, and the machine will automatically brew your espresso using the optimal temperature and extraction time.

SEMI-AUTOMATIC ESPRESSO MACHINE

This will give you a bit more control over your espresso as compared to the fully automatic. You can adjust the extraction time and you can make calibrations to perfect your espresso shot.

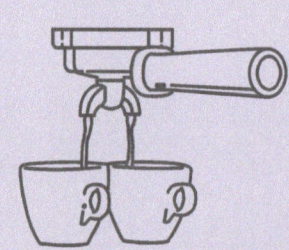

PUMP-DRIVEN ESPRESSO MACHINE (MANUAL)

This machine will give you complete control over the espresso shot for the most discerning coffee enthusiast. What you gain in control, you lose in ease and simplicity. You will need to invest time to learn techniques and in maintenance and care, but the reward will be the finest shot of espresso.

Coffee Beans

This cookbook was designed to explore different coffee recipes from around the world. While you can use any coffee bean in the following recipes, I encourage you to experiment with a variety of beans, brands, and regions. For the seasoned coffee aficionado, I invite you to experiment with new methods—palates tend to change over time, so you may make some new discoveries on your coffee journey.

COFFEE BEAN ORIGIN

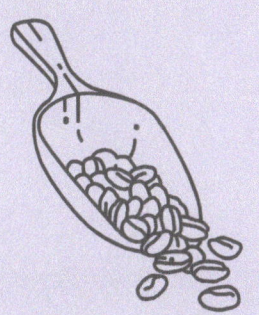

For authenticity, if you have the time and the means to seek out a variety of coffees, you will enjoy using beans that are native to the recipe's region of origin. In recipes such as the Jamaican coffee, you can easily, albeit more expensively, procure beans grown in Jamaica's Blue Mountain region. For other recipes, such as the S'mores Latte, the origin of the coffee bean is less important.

WHOLE BEANS VERSUS GROUNDS

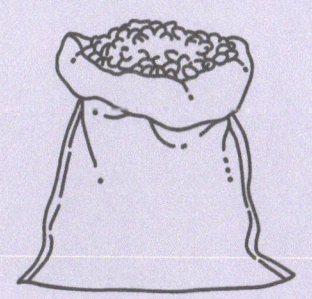

Just like with gourmet cooking, you'll always want to opt for the freshest ingredients possible. For this cookbook, I recommend using the freshest whole coffee beans possible and grinding your own beans at home just prior to brewing. Keep in mind that coffee beans in an unsealed bag become stale in less than a week. In an opaque, airtight, sealed container, coffee beans are at their best within two weeks. To make your best coffee, buy whole beans in small quantities so you can use them at their freshest and most flavorful.

HOW TO STORE COFFEE

Most coffee connoisseurs recommend storing your whole beans at room temperature in an opaque, airtight container. There is a debate about the merits of storing coffees in the freezer. I like to imagine the difference between a fresh strawberry and a once frozen strawberry: under the right conditions the flavor is similar but nothing compares to a fresh strawberry at its peak. While I prefer fresh, I'd also rather have a once-frozen strawberry than no strawberry at all. The same is true for coffee. If you must freeze your whole beans, be sure to use an airtight container.

COFFEE GRINDS

	SIZE COMPARISON	CHARACTERISTICS	RECOMMENDED USE
EXTRA COARSE	Peppercorn	Easier to filter out	Cold brew, Percolators, Stovetop
COARSE	Sea Salt	Requires longer brew time	French press
MEDIUM	Beach Sand	Most versatile	Drip coffee makers, Pour-overs
FINE	More fine than table salt	1 to 2 minute brew time	Espresso, Moka pot
EXTRA FINE	Flour	Requires boiling to extract flavor	Turkish coffees

INSTANT COFFEE

A few recipes call for instant coffee. Some instant coffees have an odd aftertaste. Be sure to experiment with different brands to find one that tastes best to you. I only use instant coffee if a recipe requires it. My preference is Folgers® instant coffee for hot brews and Starbucks® instant iced coffee for cold brews.

Milk Options

MILK AND MILK ALTERNATIVES

Many recipes call for milk as a required or optional ingredient. In all recipes, you can use your preferred milk or milk alternative. Some coffee enthusiasts recommend whole milk for the creamiest cappuccino and, indeed, dairy milks are the easiest to steam and froth. However, non-dairy milk alternatives such as soy milk and almond milk can be used throughout this book. In fact, I highly recommend oat milk for all recipes in place of whole milk. Now that I have switched to oat milk, I find that traditional dairy milk overpowers the coffee flavor. Whatever your preference, I encourage you to experiment with options and find your personal favorites.

> **I highly recommend oat milk for all recipes in place of whole milk.**

How to Steam and Froth Milk

There are several ways to steam and froth milk. While the best taste will come from using an espresso machine steaming wand, you can also steam and froth your milk with a saucepan and a whisk. Here are several options in order of the best taste and ease of preparation:

ESPRESSO MACHINE STEAMING WAND

Simply follow your espresso machine instruction manual to steam and froth your milk or milk alternative.

INSTANT AUTOMATIC ELECTRIC FROTHER

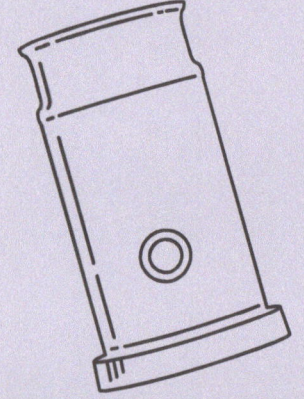

This is the easiest method and the results are very close to a manual espresso machine steaming wand. These devices are made specifically for steaming and frothing milk and typically allow you to set the milk temperature and froth style with the touch of a button.

HANDHELD ELECTRIC FROTHER

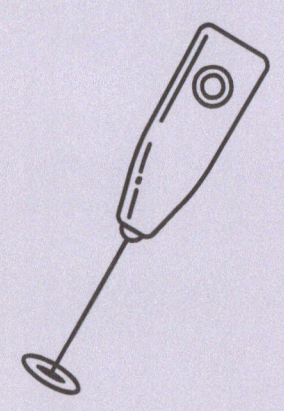

This is essentially a simple and inexpensive battery-powered whisk that serves as a good alternative to an espresso machine. Heat your milk to 150 degrees on the stovetop or in the microwave (approximately 30 seconds). The milk should be warm to the touch but not painful. Do not overheat the milk. Follow the instructions of your handheld frother to get a silky-microfoam texture.

MASON JAR

You can still steam and froth your milk without any equipment. Place milk in a mason jar without a lid and microwave for approximately 30 seconds. Remove from microwave and add lid. Shake vigorously until desired consistency (typically 30 seconds). This is an easy, inexpensive method that yields a decent tasting steamed milk.

WITH A WHISK

Heat your milk to 150 degrees on the stovetop or in the microwave (approximately 30 seconds). The milk should be warm to the touch but not painful. Do not overheat the milk. Whisk vigorously for a minute or more to desired consistency. This is more labor intensive than the above methods, but will work in a pinch.

Coffee Mugs, Cups, and Glasses

As you explore coffee recipes from around the world, I encourage you to experiment with different types of serving cups. In some cases, the recommended cup will help bolster the tasting experience and enhance the flavors presented. In some cases, the suggested cup will simply add to the adventure by making your experience more authentic to the recipe's origin. Each recipe will recommend a specific serving glass, which will often, but not always, match the accompanying photograph. However, you're also encouraged to improvise with the glassware you have readily available.

Homemade Whipped Cream

Many recipes within this book call for whipped cream. You can use store-bought whipped cream, but making it at home is easy and exponentially more flavorful and decadent.

INSTRUCTIONS

Using an electric mixer, whisk whipping cream until frothy. Add vanilla and confectioners sugar. Continue to whisk until stiff peaks form. The stiff peaks stage is reached when the peaks stand straight up when you lift the mixer out of the cream. Do not overmix or the whipped cream will lose its smooth texture. Store any unused whipped cream in the refrigerator for up to three days.

Pro tip: If using a metal bowl, chill the bowl first which will help you reach the stiff peaks stage faster.

TIME
5 minutes

EQUIPMENT
Electric mixer

INGREDIENTS
1 cup heavy whipping cream
1 tsp vanilla
1 Tbsp confectioners sugar

DEMITASSE CUP
2 - 3 OUNCES

DOUBLE ESPRESSO CUP
2 - 4 OUNCES

STANDARD CERAMIC
COFFEE MUG
8 - 10 OUNCES

STANDARD GLASS COFFEE CUP
(DOUBLE WALLED
RECOMMENDED) 8 - 10 OUNCES

CAPPUCCINO
5 - 6 OUNCES

LATTE MUG
12 - 15 OUNCES

GLASS TUMBLER
10 - 12 OUNCES

GLASS IRISH COFFEE MUG
10 - 12 OUNCES

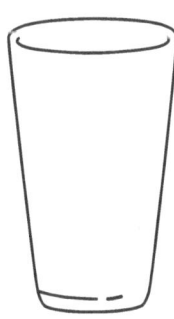

TALL GLASS
14 - 16 OUNCES

MASON JAR
8 - 14 OUNCES

COFFEE RECIPES

AFFOGATO IN FLORENCE

The word affogato means "drowning" in Italian so we will drown our vanilla ice cream in a rich espresso. While you could add whipped cream, chocolate sauce, or a dash of cinnamon, an affogato is already perfection so I recommend serving it with just these two simple ingredients.

INSTRUCTIONS

Prepare a double shot of espresso. Place vanilla ice cream in a coffee mug or small bowl. Slowly pour espresso over vanilla ice cream and serve immediately.

LOCATION

Florence, Italy

TIME

5 minutes

EQUIPMENT

Espresso machine

INGREDIENTS

2 shots espresso

1 scoop vanilla ice cream

AIRPLANE COFFEE

LOCATION

The friendly skies

TIME

5 minutes

EQUIPMENT

Any coffee brewer

INGREDIENTS

2 cups of strongly brewed coffee

1 single serve creamer (optional)

1 single serve sugar packet (optional)

1 single serve Biscoff cookie (not optional!)

Fasten your seatbelts! Today's coffee brings us 36,000 feet in the air to experience airplane coffee, made with absurdly hot coffee in a paper cup and Biscoff cookies. As we explore coffee recipes from around the world, our journey would not be complete without a sample of airplane coffee, which is always served at extremely hot temperatures. So grab your favorite book, your passport, and headphones as we prepare a cup of in-flight coffee.

INSTRUCTIONS

Brew your favorite cup of coffee, then heat it in the microwave for 2 minutes. Caution! Your coffee will be extremely hot. Just like on an airplane, you will have to read a few more pages of your book and patiently wait at least five minutes for your coffee to cool to a reasonable temperature. Once your coffee stops steaming, sip slowly and carefully. Then, chug the rest of the coffee because the flight attendant is coming around to pick up all remaining cups and glasses before landing.

Ladies and gentlemen, as we start our descent, please make sure your seat backs and tray tables are in their full upright position. Make sure your seat belt is securely fastened and all carry-on luggage is stowed underneath the seat in front of you or in the overhead bins. We will soon be landing in a new city, where a new coffee experience awaits you!

ARABIC COFFEE IN ABU DHABI

In the United Arab Emirates you will see images of the traditional dallah, an Arabic coffee pot, depicted in civic art and on their dirham coin. Using a dallah, lightly roasted coffee is boiled with cardamom, cloves, saffron, rose water, or a combination thereof. It is frequently served with nuts or dates.

INSTRUCTIONS

In a dallah or a small saucepan, bring water and sugar (if using) to a boil. Remove from heat. Add coffee, cardamom, and cloves. Add saffron and rose water (if using). Return saucepan to stovetop and bring to a boil again. Once coffee begins to foam, remove from heat. Return saucepan to stovetop for a third and final time; bring to a boil. Remove from heat. Carefully pour into a demitasse cup, which is called a fenjan in Arabic, to preserve the foam layer. Sip slowly to avoid ingesting any coffee grounds or cloves which should settle at the bottom of the cup.

LOCATION
Abu Dhabi, UAE

TIME
10 minutes

EQUIPMENT
Dallah (an Arabic coffee pot) or a standard saucepan

INGREDIENTS
1 cup water
1 tsp sugar (optional)
1 Tbsp finely ground coffee
⅛ tsp ground cardamom or crushed cardamom pod
1 tsp whole cloves
1 saffron thread (optional)
1 Tbsp rose water (optional)

BULLETPROOF COFFEE IN SILICON VALLEY

LOCATION

Silicon Valley, California

TIME

8 minutes

EQUIPMENT

Any coffee brewer and a blender

INGREDIENTS

1 cup brewed coffee

1 Tbsp MCT oil

1 Tbsp grass-fed unsalted butter or ghee

Our coffee trip today brings us to Silicon Valley for a Bulletproof Coffee.™ In 2004 Dave Asprey, the founder of Bulletproof Coffee, had an energizing and healing cup of yak butter tea in Tibet. That led him on a journey to create science-based products to improve weight loss, energy level, and brain function.

Some advocates tout Bulletproof products' ability to stave off hunger, amplify laser sharp focus, and lift brain fog. Others are skeptical of its effects and encourage caution, considering a Bulletproof coffee has 250 to 450 calories and saturated fats.

MCT oil is a medium-chain triglyceride made from coconut oil. Bulletproof sells their MCT oil labeled as a "Brain Octane Oil" but there are also generic options available. Experts recommend starting with 1 teaspoon of MCT oil added to your coffee and working your way up to 2 tablespoons over a few days.

It's surprisingly good! I started enjoying this daily for a few weeks and loved the boost and the taste.

INSTRUCTIONS

Using a blender, combine all ingredients until frothy. Pour into a mug and be surprised by the delicious creaminess!

CAFFÈ AMERICANO IN THE USA

History suggests that the Caffè Americano was invented during WWII. American soldiers stationed in Italy were not yet partial to the strong flavors of an espresso. To adapt, hot water was added to dilute the espresso. The easiest way to distinguish a Caffè Americano from a black cup of coffee (other than taste) is that the Caffè Americano retains a small layer of espresso crema on top.

INSTRUCTIONS

Heat water to near boiling in a teapot or saucepan. Meanwhile, prepare two shots espresso. Add hot water to a standard coffee mug. Slowly pour espresso into the water taking care to keep the crema intact as the top layer.

> *While the Caffè Americano originated in Italy, it was created to accommodate an American palate. In May 2020, I was experimenting with coffee global coffee recipes. During this same period, George Floyd was murdered by a police officer during an arrest over a supposed twenty dollar counterfeit bill. The incident was recorded by a bystander and sparked an outrage throughout the country. Amidst national-wide protests against police brutality, I pondered the meaning of being American, which led me to alter the Caffè Americano recipe and photograph to reflect my respect for social justice and diversity.*

LOCATION

America

TIME

5 minutes

EQUIPMENT

Espresso machine

INGREDIENTS

1 cup water

2 shots espresso

1 part social justice

Equal parts diversity, equity, and inclusion

A dash of civil disobedience

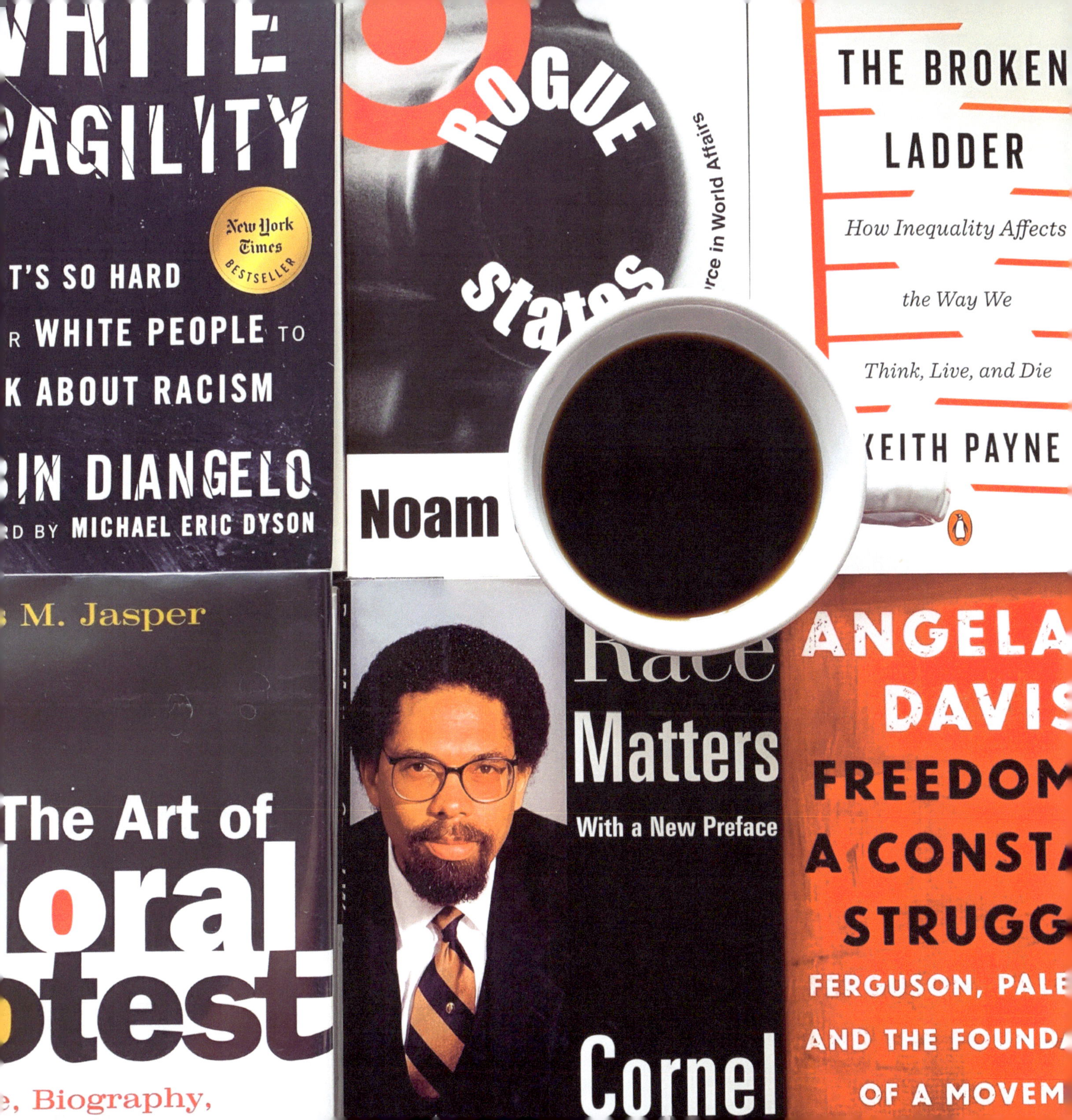
HITE
AGILITY
New York Times BESTSELLER
T'S SO HARD
R WHITE PEOPLE TO
K ABOUT RACISM
IN DIANGELO
D BY MICHAEL ERIC DYSON
ROGUE
States
rce in World Affairs
Noam
THE BROKEN
LADDER
How Inequality Affects
the Way We
Think, Live, and Die
KEITH PAYNE
M. Jasper
The Art of
oral
otest
e, Biography,
Race
Matters
With a New Preface
Cornel
ANGELA
DAVIS
FREEDOM
A CONST
STRUGG
FERGUSON, PALE
AND THE FOUND
OF A MOVEM

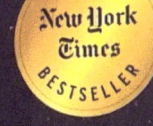

CAFÉ AU LAIT IN PARIS

LOCATION

Paris, France

TIME

5 minutes

EQUIPMENT

French press or any coffee brewer and a milk steamer

INGREDIENTS

1 cup strongly brewed coffee

1 cup milk

We are going to France today with a Café Au Lait! References to Café Au Lait appear in letters dating as far back as the 17th century, which coincides with the first Parisian cafés that opened in the 1670s. By 1723 there were 323 cafés in Paris and more than 1,800 by 1790. One of the most well-known cafés, Les Deux Magots, is still open today and was frequented by Simone de Beauvoir, Pablo Picasso, Jean-Paul Sartre, and Ernest Hemingway.

INSTRUCTIONS

Brew one cup of coffee. Steam milk using your preferred method (see page 26). Combine coffee and steamed milk in a large ceramic mug. Sip and imagine you're in an outdoor Parisian café planning your afternoon trip to the Lourve.

CAFÉ CON MIEL IN VALENCIA

This Spanish coffee is sweetened with honey. The earliest evidence of foraging for honey is depicted in cave paintings in Cuevas de la Araña in Spain dating back 8,000 years. We're making a latte version today, but you can also add milk and honey to a regular cup of coffee too. We're pairing this with traditional Spanish cookies called polvorones. With only five ingredients, they are easy to make and crumble-in-your-mouth delicious! They are a lovely accompaniment to the Café con Miel.

INSTRUCTIONS

Brew two shots of espresso. Steam milk using the wand on your espresso machine or one of the alternative options mentioned on page 26. In a latte cup, combine espresso and steamed milk. Stir in honey and vanilla. Sprinkle cinnamon on top and enjoy!

LOCATION

Valencia, Spain

TIME

5 minutes

EQUIPMENT

Espresso machine or French press

INGREDIENTS

2 shots of espresso

½ cup steamed milk

1 Tbsp honey

⅛ tsp vanilla

⅛ tsp cinnamon

CAFÉ CUBANO IN HAVANA

LOCATION

Havana, Cuba

TIME

5 minutes

EQUIPMENT

Espresso machine

INGREDIENTS

1 shot espresso

1 Tbsp granulated sugar

The Café Cubano is an espresso sweetened with sugar that has been whipped into a creamy froth with the most decadent drops of espresso. I'm daydreaming that I'm in Baracoa, the oldest city in Cuba, known for black sand beaches, peaceful rivers, waterfalls, palm trees, and lush forests.

INSTRUCTIONS

Prepare one shot of espresso. Working quickly to preserve the temperature and freshness, whisk 1 tablespoon espresso with sugar in a small bowl until creamy. Pour into an espresso cup, then slowly add in remaining espresso. Aim to have a rich sugar froth at the bottom of the cup, followed by the espresso, and a thick layer of crema on top. The magic is in the layers. Be sure to sip slowly and notice how the flavor profile changes as you encounter each layer.

CAFÉ DE OLLA IN MEXICO CITY

Today's coffee trip brings us to Mexico - one of my favorite countries in the world. Café de Olla originated during the Mexican Revolution, when hardworking women joined the war effort by carrying supplies, providing meals, and serving a nourishing and energizing blend of coffee that has become known as Café de Olla, made with coffee, piloncillo (a solid unrefined whole cane sugar also known as panela), and cinnamon.

It is exquisite and comforting - if you haven't tried this yet, I think you're missing out!

INSTRUCTIONS

In a medium saucepan over low heat, stir water, panela, and cinnamon stick until sugar is dissolved (about 5 minutes). Increase to high heat until boiling. Add coffee grounds and remove from heat. Cover and let steep for 5 minutes. Strain, serve, and savor!

LOCATION

Mexico City, Mexico

TIME

10 minutes

EQUIPMENT

Saucepan

INGREDIENTS

2 cups water

¼ cup panela (or brown sugar)

½ stick cinnamon

2 Tbsp ground coffee

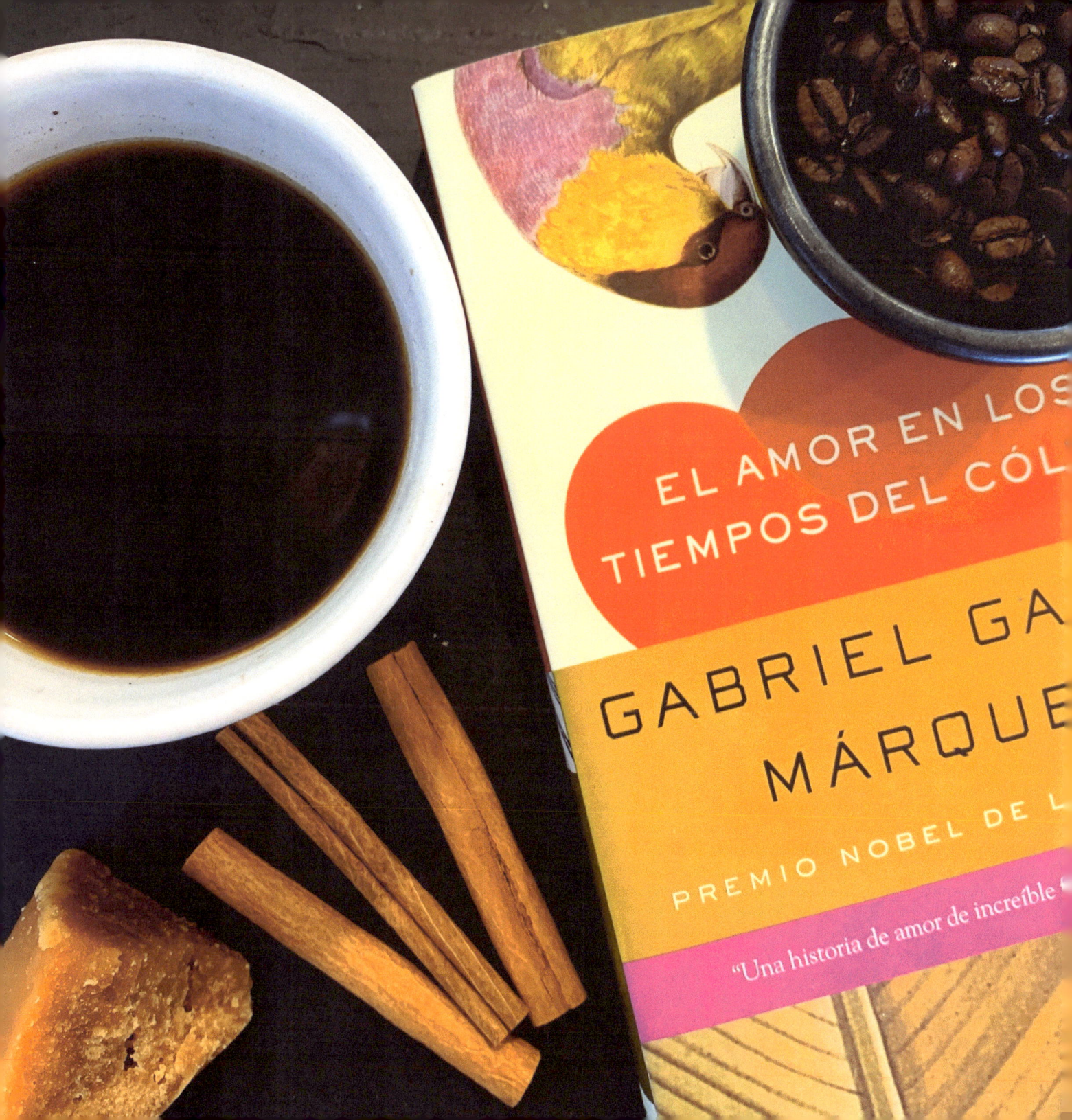

CAFE HAFUCH IN TEL AVIV

LOCATION

Tel Aviv, Israel

TIME

5 minutes

EQUIPMENT

Espresso machine

INGREDIENTS

1 cup milk (and extra for additional microfoam as needed)

2 shots espresso

Coffee culture has blossomed in Israel over the last few decades. One of the more popular coffees served in Israeli coffeeshops is the Cafe Hafuch, which is essentially an upside-down cappuccino..

INSTRUCTIONS

Steam milk and pour into a tall glass. Separately, prepare a double shot of espresso. Using a spoon resting just above the steamed milk, slowly pour in your espresso, being careful to preserve the layers. Prepare additional milk froth and spoon it gently on top of the espresso layer. The timing is tricky on this one. I recommend having all your tools, equipment, and ingredients prepped and organized in advance so you can easily assemble the steamed milk, bubbly froth, and espresso at their best temperatures.

CAFÉ MOCHA IN MOKHA

The term mocha comes from the coastal town of Mokha in Yemen. In the early 15th century, Mokha was the epicenter of the coffee trade. The word mocha became interchangeable with the word coffee and some say the coffee beans had a rich chocolate flavor. However, at some point, real chocolate was added to coffee leading to today's interpretation of a Café Mocha. Some say the tradition began in Italy or France, and others say the name, but likely not the recipe, was coined in America.

INSTRUCTIONS

Brew one cup of coffee. Meanwhile heat milk and chocolate over medium heat in small saucepan. Stir frequently until chocolate is completely melted and incorporated into milk. Combine coffee, chocolate milk, and sugar in a large ceramic mug or a tall coffee glass. Top with whipped cream and chocolate syrup.

LOCATION

Mokha, Yemen

TIME

10 minutes

EQUIPMENT

Any coffee brewer

INGREDIENTS

1 cup brewed coffee

½ cup milk

4 Tbsp high quality dark or milk chocolate

1 Tbsp sugar

Homemade whipped cream (page 28)

Chocolate syrup for garnish

CAPPUCCINO IN MILAN

LOCATION

Milan, Italy

TIME

10 minutes

EQUIPMENT

Espresso machine

INGREDIENTS

2 shots espresso

½ cup milk for steaming and froth

Although the name "kapuziner" was used in Viennese coffee shops in the 1700s, the term referred to a simple coffee with cream and sugar. The cappuccino as we know it today was invented in Italy after the first espresso machine was patented in 1901 by Luigi Bezzera. Cappuccinos are made with good espresso, steamed milk, and frothed milk.

INSTRUCTIONS

Prepare two shots of espresso. Steam milk using the wand on your espresso machine or one of the alternative options mentioned on page 26. Aim to create a smooth, sweet milk with an abundant amount of froth. Place espresso in a ceramic mug. Slowly pour in steamed milk and top with a thick layer of milk froth.

CHARCOAL COFFEE IN CAIRO

Today we are making an activated charcoal espresso latte from Egypt. The first documented use of charcoal was recorded in 3750 BC in Egypt to melt and combine metals. Around 1500 BC, the Egyptians began using charcoal for medicinal purposes and later to treat and filter water.

INSTRUCTIONS

Add milk, charcoal, espresso, maple syrup, and vanilla into a glass mug and stir gently to combine. Use a glass mug so you can see the striking color of the charcoal while sipping on your Egyptian delicacy!

> *Today people claim there are health benefits to consuming activated charcoal, but there is little evidence in support. Activated charcoal is often used to treat severe poisoning since it helps prevent the poison from being absorbed into the stomach. A tiny amount in a coffee drink is likely harmless, but I wouldn't make it a habit. In larger doses it could prevent the absorption of important nutrients or medications. I'm obsessed with the color, and it tastes like a regular delicious latte!*

LOCATION

Cairo, Egypt

TIME

8 minutes

EQUIPMENT

Espresso machine

INGREDIENTS

1 cup milk

1 tsp food grade activated charcoal

1 shot espresso

1 tsp maple syrup

1 tsp vanilla

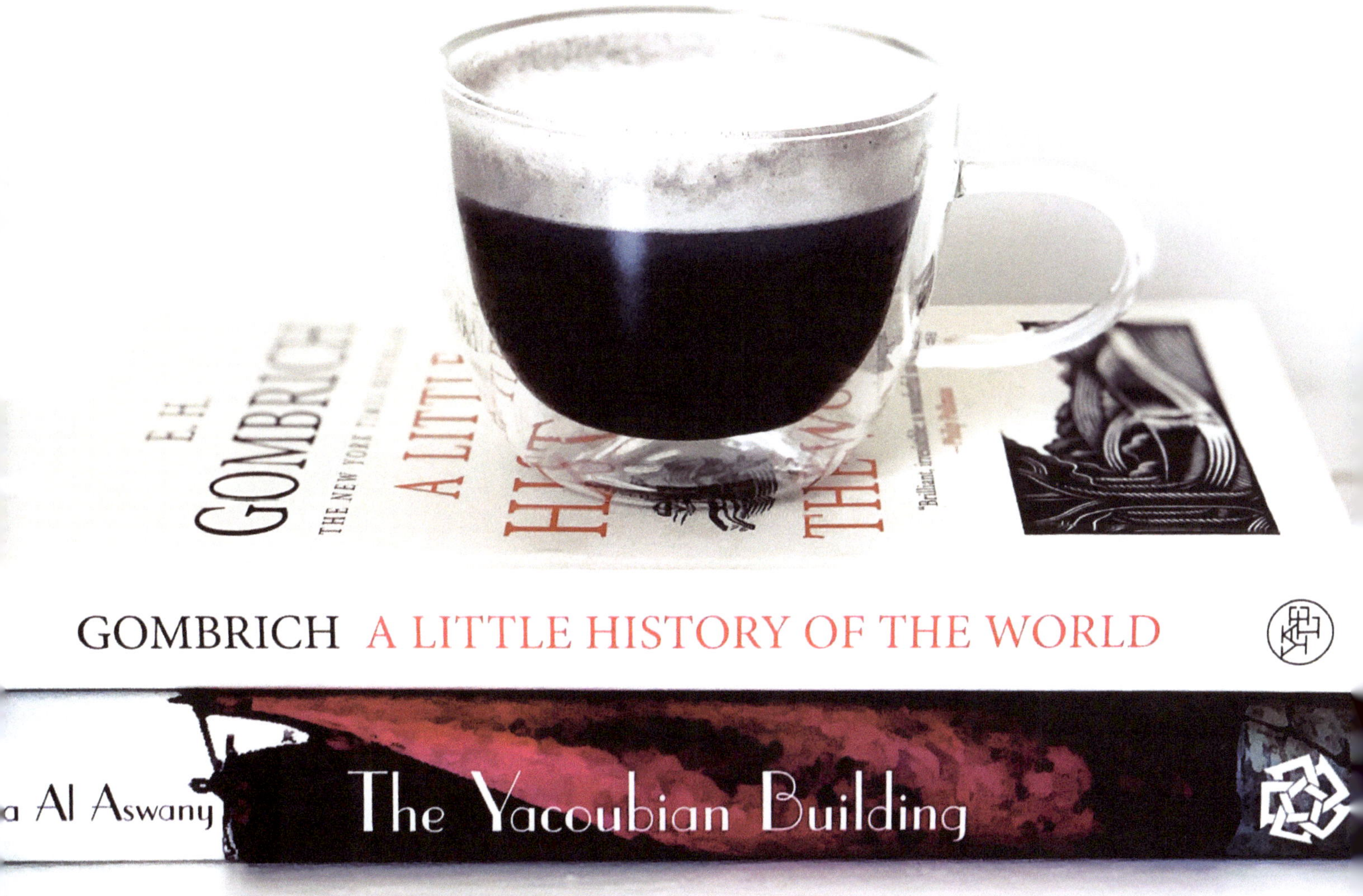

GOMBRICH A LITTLE HISTORY OF THE WORLD

CHICORY CAFÉ AU LAIT IN NEW ORLEANS

DESTINATION

New Orleans, Louisiana

TIME

5 minutes

EQUIPMENT

French press

INGREDIENTS

1 Tbsp chicory grounds

3 Tbsp coffee, coarsely ground

1½ cups hot water

1 cup warm milk

The harvesting of the chicory root began in ancient Egypt. Later, during Napoleon's blockades from 1807 to 1811, coffee supplies were hard to come by. The French roasted, ground, and brewed the root of the chicory plant using it as a coffee replacement or to stretch their limited coffee supply. The practice reappeared later New Orleans, a city founded by the French. During the civil war, coffee once again became a scarce resource and the French practice of using the chicory root made a resurgence. While coffee is abundant now, chicory coffee has become a tradition especially in New Orleans at the famous Café du Monde. Pair your chicory coffee with a fresh stack of homemade beignets!

INSTRUCTIONS

In a French press, combine chicory grounds and coffee grounds. Add hot water and steep for five minutes. Combine brewed chicory coffee with equal parts hot milk.

Preheat French press by adding hot water, swirling, then discarding water. Boil hot water, remove from heat and set aside for 30 seconds. This will bring your water to the recommended temperature of 195 - 205 degrees fahrenheit. Place chicory grounds and coffee grounds in French press. Pour in just enough hot water to cover the grounds. Stir once to ensure grounds are properly immersed in water. Let sit for 30 seconds allowing coffee to bloom. Add remaining hot water. Add lid but do not depress plunger. Let steep for exactly 4 minutes. Slowly lower the plunger. Pour into a large mug, add warm milk, and enjoy!

COCONUT MILK COFFEE IN KONA

Hawai'i is known for growing premium Kona coffee beans, derived from Brazilian cuttings introduced to the Kona region in the early 1800s. Our second featured ingredient is the coconut, which was likely introduced to Hawai'i by Polynesian settlers. We are combining coffee with coconut to make two different concoctions. First, we're adding coconut milk to coffee and topping it with coconut whipped cream. Second, we're complementing this with a coffee panna cotta!

INSTRUCTIONS

Chill coconut milk in refrigerator for 24 hours. The next day carefully separate thickened, solid coconut milk from coconut liquid. Reserve the liquid for another purpose such as a curry dish, cocktail, or dessert. Place solid coconut milk in a medium bowl and whip with a hand mixer until soft peaks form.

Brew your favorite cup of coffee and stir in 2 tablespoons coconut milk. Place a heap of whipped coconut cream atop your coffee and garnish with shredded coconut. Sip and enjoy the aloha spirit!

LOCATION
Kona, Hawai'i

TIME
10 minutes

EQUIPMENT
Any coffee brewer

INGREDIENTS
1 cup brewed coffee

2 Tbsp coconut milk

1 can full fat coconut milk (not light)

1 Tbsp shredded coconut (optional for garnish)

COFFEE AND COLA FLOAT IN RIO DE JANEIRO

DESTINATION

Rio de Janeiro, Brazil

TIME

8 minutes

EQUIPMENT

Any coffee brewer

INGREDIENTS

½ cup chilled extra strongly brewed coffee

½ can cola

1 cup chocolate milk

Homemade whipped cream (optional)

1 scoop vanilla ice cream (optional but highly recommended)

Chocolate syrup (optional)

The coffee plant was brought to Brazil in the early 18th century and coffee became Brazil's largest export by 1820. The country's most common coffee is a "cafezinho," a small, intense shot of pure black coffee served with sugar. In 2020 Coca-Cola announced it would introduce a "Coca-Cola with coffee" that combines regular Coke with Brazilian coffee to the US market in 2021. Let's explore by making a Brazilian Coffee Cola Float!

INSTRUCTIONS

Combine coffee, cola, and chocolate milk in a 12 ounce tall glass or mason jar. Add ice cubes as desired. Top with homemade whipped cream, ice cream, or both! Drizzle with chocolate syrup and enjoy.

COFFEE JELLY IN BATANGAS

The first coffee tree was planted as early as 1730 in Batangas, and today the Philippines is one of only a few countries that grows four varieties of coffee: Arabica, Liberica (Barako), Excelsa, and Robusta. While coffee jelly was featured in English cookbooks in the 1800s, it has recently become popular again in Japan. We're making a Filipino version today with sweetened condensed milk. I substituted the gelatin with agar powder to make it vegetarian.

INSTRUCTIONS

In a small bowl, combine the gelatin powder and 4 tablespoons of water. Set aside. In a saucepan over medium heat, bring coffee and sugar to a near boil, stirring occasionally. Remove from heat and add in gelatin mixture. Stir until gelatin mix dissolves. Let cool slightly then pour into a shallow baking 8x8 baking dish and refrigerate until completely set (at least 6 hours). Meanwhile, in a small bowl, combine sweetened condensed milk with light whipping cream and set in the refrigerator to chill. Once the jelly has set, cut into ½ inch cubes. Spoon cube into individual serving dishes, and top with the chilled milk mixture.

DESTINATION
Batangas, Philippines

TIME
Prep time 15 minutes; wait time 6 hours

EQUIPMENT
Any coffee brewer

SERVES 4

INGREDIENTS
1 Tbsp gelatin powder (for vegetarians, use agar agar)

4 Tbsp water

2 cups brewed coffee, at room temperature

2 Tbsp sugar

1 14 oz can sweetened condensed milk

1 cup light whipping cream or milk

CHAPTER 11

Bombay.

Such a deceptive word, so soft-sounding, like sponge cake in the mouth. Even the new name for the city, Mumbai, carries that round softness, so that a visitor is unprepared for the reality of this giant, bewildering city, which is an assault, a punch in the face. Everything about the city attacks you at once, as you leave the green tranquillity of the surrounding hills and enter it—the rows of slums that look like something built for and by giant, erratic birds rather than humans; the old, crumbling buildings that have not seen a lick of paint in decades and many of which are held up by scaffoldings; the new, tall buildings that rise from the wretched streets and point like thin fingers toward a dirty, polluted sky; the insane tango of auto rickshaws and cars and bicycles and scooters and bullock carts competing for their inch of space, creating their riotous din of blaring horns and yells and invective; the beggars—armless, legless, fingerless, eyeless, and the lepers, dear God, even noseless—darting in between the vehicles, the legless ones perched on a homemade skateboard, making it hard for the drivers to spot them; and above all, the people, the constant, ever-present mass of people, thousands of them on every street, spilling from the slum-invaded sidewalks

by it, an... humanity in motion. Y... urbs, which have none of the green 'burbs, and pass street after street of selling everything from jeans to gold jew... leaf concoction known as *paan*, which eve... class background seems to chew. Occasion... name you recognize—Sony, Wrangler, No... not to notice the billboards that say Coke or Wars being fought across the country. But mo... because your attention is pulled in multiple dire... coming up to your right and about to hit your to control your reaction, bite down on your tong... minute yell to Satish to watch out and feel the quie... rassment when the taxi misses your car by inches— seem to—and Satish flashes you a grin in the rearvie... here you are stopped at a traffic light and your car by scores of tired-looking young women with child hips, beating on the windows with their open hands as money, and you feel hot and flushed and don't know whe... know it is dangerous to make eye contact but staring strai... feels pretty untenable, also, and on top of this Satish is ad... ing you not to weaken, not to toss out a few coins because th... always more beggars than coins. So you sit in your air-condit... car, ignoring the sound of hands beating on the window, feeling... a chimp in a zoo, remembering that other time a couple of mon... ago when other, angrier hands had beaten on your car, feeling th... lethal combination of pity and aggravation that India always seem... to arouse in you. And then, at the last minute, you sense that your wife can't take this anymore and she reaches into her purse for a few one-rupee coins and, watching this, the crowd outside your car gets frantic, you can feel it even though you're safely inside, and suddenly

---

MANIL SURI

...EATH OF VISHNU

COFFEE LASSI IN MUMBAI

DESTINATION

Mumbai, India

TIME

5 minutes prep time, plus 30 minutes to chill espresso in advance

EQUIPMENT

Espresso machine and blender

INGREDIENTS

1 shot espresso, chilled

1/3 cup plain yogurt

1/2 cup milk

4 cardamom pods, crushed

1 medjool date, pit removed

1 tsp honey

The lassi is ubiquitous in India and is almost always made with yogurt, water, and sugar. While lassis are enjoyed year-round, they are particularly savored in the heat of the summer months. The most common variation is the Mango Lassi, which is now served in many countries around the world. Our cafe version combines coffee, cardamom, and yogurt – it is simply divine and refreshing. Someday I'll sip a coffee lassi then explore the Elephanta Caves, a UNESCO World Heritage Site in Mumbai.

INSTRUCTIONS

Blend chilled espresso, yogurt, milk, cardamom pods, a medjool date, and one teaspoon honey. Pour through a fine-meshed sieve and serve over ice in a tall 12 ounce glass. I hope you've discovered one of your new favorite coffee drinks!

COFFEE LIQUEUR IN VERACRUZ

The most popular coffee Liqueur originated in Mexico's beautiful Veracruz in 1936. It takes a few days to make but the results are worth it. There are so many variations to this recipe which means you can't go wrong. Have fun and experiment. ¡Salud!

INSTRUCTIONS

Carefully cut open vanilla pods lengthwise. Stir together coffee grounds, vodka or rum, and split-open vanilla bean pods. Place in a mason jar or airtight container. Refrigerate and shake occasionally for two days. Using a fine-mesh stainer, filter liquid and discard coffee grounds and vanilla pods. In a saucepan over low heat, simmer water and brown sugar for five minutes, stirring frequently until sugar is fully dissolved. Combine sugar syrup with the coffee-vanilla-infused liqueur. Serve over ice. Or, make a White Russian (see page 154) or a Jamaican Rum and Coffee (see page 107).

DESTINATION

Veracruz, Mexico

TIME

8 minutes prep; 48 hours wait time

EQUIPMENT

Saucepan

INGREDIENTS

½ cup coarsely ground coffee beans

2 cups vodka or rum

2 vanilla pods

4 cups water

2 cups brown sugar

COLD BREW IN TOKYO

DESTINATION

Tokyo, Japan

TIME

12 hours

EQUIPMENT

Fine mesh sieve and paper filter

SERVES 4

INGREDIENTS

1 cup coarsely ground coffee

4 cups water, room temperature

4 cups water, cold

There is evidence that tea leaves were steeped using cold river water in Japan in the 1600s. No hot water was required; just patience and time. Around the same time, Dutch traders were making concentrated coffee to bring aboard long voyages to avoid the risk that brewing with an open flame would have on a flammable wooden ship. I like to imagine that a Dutch trader and a Japanese buyer sat together surrounded by crates of silk, porcelain, and silver. They exchanged their life stories along with secrets on brewing tea and making concentrated coffee and thus began a brand new tradition. Like so many of our coffee recipes, the genesis of this coffee is the offspring of long journeys and cultural exchanges.

INSTRUCTIONS

Combine 1 cup coarsely ground coffee with 4 cups room temperature water. Let steep 12 hours at room temperature. Filter out the coffee grounds using a fine mesh sieve. Filter once more using a paper filter or cheesecloth. Combine 1 cup concentrated cold brew with 1 cup cold water. Serve over ice. Milk and sugar optional.

> **On page 103, we made a Japanese iced coffee by simply pouring hot water over coffee grounds. The hot water then cascaded directly into a reservoir of ice using a Chemex pour-over. Today we are following a traditional slow brew process by steeping ground coffee in water overnight.**

CORTADO IN BASQUE COUNTRY

The elegant cortado, from the Basque Country of Northern Spain, is made with equal parts espresso and steamed milk. The milk is neither frothy nor texturized as it's meant to "cut through" (cortado) just enough to reduce the bitterness but maintain the richness of the espresso shot. Let's pair this coffee with a book from Federico García Lorca, a Spanish poet, playwright, and theater director whose influence brought on the Golden Age of Spanish theater.

INSTRUCTIONS

Prepare a double shot of espresso in a 4 oz coffee cup. Prepare steamed milk with very little froth. Pour milk into espresso. Sip and savor a taste of Spain!

DESTINATION
Basque Country, Spain

TIME
5 minutes

EQUIPMENT
Espresso machine

INGREDIENTS
2 shots espresso
¼ cup steamed milk

DALGONA COFFEE IN SEOUL

DESTINATION

Seoul, South Korea

TIME

10 minutes

EQUIPMENT

Handmixer

INGREDIENTS

2 Tbsp granulated sugar

2 Tbsp instant coffee granules

2 Tbsp boiling water

1 cup milk of choice

The Dalgona coffee originated in India, Pakistan, and Macau. However, it only rose to global fame when a Korean actor noted the resemblance between Dalgona coffee and a popular Korean sponge candy. The coffee quickly became a viral trend on TikTok. The whipped coffee has a strong, harsh flavor but when mixed in with the milk, it's delicious.

INSTRUCTIONS

In a small bowl using a hand mixer, beat sugar, coffee and hot water until thick and creamy, and soft peaks begin to form (about 3 to 5 minutes). Fill a glass cup or mason jar with ice. Add milk leaving at least ½ inch at the top of the glass to add whipped coffee. Using a spoon, add whipped coffee to top of milk and pile high to make soft peaks. Take your Instagram photo then mix well before enjoying this delicious treat!

EGGNOG LATTE IN LONDON

While there is a lively debate on the lineage of eggnog, most agree it was likely derived from the British drink "posset" made with ale, eggs, and figs. Across the pond, American colonists started making eggnog with Caribbean rum. In Mexico, the addition of cinnamon and rum is called a Rompope. In Peru, the creamy dessert drink, Algarrobina, is made with eggnog, pisco, and algarrobina (black carob syrup).

DESTINATION

London, England

TIME

15 minutes

EQUIPMENT

Any coffee brewer

INGREDIENTS FOR EGGNOG

3 egg yolks

½ cup granulated sugar

½ cup heavy whipping cream

1 cup milk

2 tsp nutmeg

INGREDIENTS FOR EGGNOG LATTE

1 cup eggnog

1 cup brewed coffee

Some baristas call for espresso but I found it overpowers the eggnog. If you've never had homemade eggnog, you will definitely want to try this. Best. Eggnog. Ever. It's decadent!

INSTRUCTIONS

PREPARE THE EGGNOG

Using a hand mixer or a whisk, whisk together egg yolks and sugar until light and creamy. Set aside. Meanwhile in a saucepan over medium heat, stir together heavy whipping cream, milk, and nutmeg. Stir constantly and bring to a high simmer but do not boil. Take ⅓ cup of warm milk mixture and add to egg bowl; whisk vigorously. Add another ⅓ cup warm milk to egg bowl; whisk vigorously. Repeat until most of milk mixture has been added to egg bowl, then pour entire bowl back into the saucepan. Stir constantly for 3 minutes until slightly thickened. Remove from heat. Stir in 1 tsp vanilla. Set aside one cup eggnog for your latte; put remaining eggnog in container and store in refrigerator to use for tomorrow's latte or tonight's fireside rum cocktail.

MAKE THE LATTE

Stir together 1 cup coffee with 1 cup eggnog. Top with homemade whipped cream and sprinkled cinnamon.

EINSPÄNNER IN VIENNA

DESTINATION

Vienna, Austria

TIME

8 minutes

EQUIPMENT

Espresso machine

INGREDIENTS

1 shot espresso

2 Tbsp homemade whipped cream (see page 28)

Made with espresso and whipped cream, the Einspänner is also known as an espresso con panna in Italy and a Café Viennois in the UK and France. As long as we're imagining sipping a coffee in Vienna, let's also imagine a visit to the Schönbrunn Palace where Mozart, age 6, played for Empress Maria Theresa in 1762.

INSTRUCTIONS

Prepare one shot of espresso in a demitasse cup. Gently spoon whipped cream on top of espresso. Serve immediately. Sometimes the most perfect moments are made from two simple ingredients!

Like many recipes in this book, you may want to double the recipe. This is such a delicious drink that you will likely want seconds!

ES ALPUKAT IN JAKARTA

Es Alpukat, or ice avocado, is sold by street vendors and restaurants across Indonesia. It can be served as a bowl of layered ingredients or blended, often served with chocolate ice cream, milo powder (chocolate malt), or chocolate syrup. I love all the recipes within this book, but this one stands out as one of the absolute best.

INSTRUCTIONS

Blend together all ingredients until smooth. This will only take about 30 seconds to 1 minute. Optional: coat inside of glass with chocolate syrup. Pour into a 12 ounce tall glass or mason jar and enjoy!

DESTINATION

Jakarta, Indonesia

TIME

5 minutes

EQUIPMENT

Blender

INGREDIENTS

½ ripe avocado

1 cup strongly brewed coffee

2 tsp vanilla

2 ice cubes

½ cup sweetened condensed milk

Chocolate syrup for topping (optional)

ESPRESSO IN MILAN

DESTINATION

Milan, Italy

TIME

5 minutes

EQUIPMENT

Espresso machine

INGREDIENTS

18 - 21 grams espresso beans, finely ground

38 - 42 ml water

In 1906, Luigi Bezzera and Desiderio Pavoni introduced their espresso machine at the World's Fair in Milan. Now espresso is enjoyed around the world and serves as the base for many of the recipes within this book.

If you're a coffee connoisseur, you likely already have your favorite method and espresso machine. If you're new to espresso, I encourage you to experiment and explore the many options espresso offers. Before creating this book, I wasn't partial to espresso. Now I savor every sip.

INSTRUCTIONS

There are many different types of espresso machines that range from simple one-button automatic machines to elaborate manual machines that allow you to control water flow, temperature, and many other details. I have a De'Longhi Dedica DeLuxe Semi-Automatic Espresso Machine that allows me to make a few adjustments but is relatively easy to learn.

While there are many options, a typical double shot of espresso is made with 18 to 21 grams of fine grounds using 38 to 42 ml of water at a temperature of 200° brewed for 25 to 30 seconds. For the best results, follow your espresso machine's instructions. Once you have the basics mastered, you can experiment with additional options, such as the ones featured on page 140.

ESPRESSO MARTINI IN SYDNEY

Legend has it that the first espresso martini was made in London at the SoHo Brasserie in 1983 when a supermodel asked for a drink that would "wake her up and f*ck her up." The drink caught on and jumped continents. According to Mr. Black Coffee Liqueur, the espresso martini is the highest-selling cocktail in Australian bars. And the espresso martini rose to #7 on the list of most popular cocktails worldwide in 2019. I recommend using Mr. Black Coffee Liqueur, which is roasted, distilled, and bottled in Australia.

INSTRUCTIONS

Using a cocktail shaker, combine Mr. Black Coffee Liqueur, espresso, and ice cubes. Shake vigorously to create a significant froth. Pour into a chilled coupe glass. Add a splash of milk or whipping cream as desired. Garnish with three coffee beans.

> *Let's pair this espresso martini with the traditional cake of Australia - the Lamington! Who doesn't love a vanilla cake layered with strawberry filling and dipped in chocolate?!?*

DESTINATION
Sydney, Australia

TIME
5 minutes

EQUIPMENT
Espresso machine

INGREDIENTS
2 shots Mr. Black Coffee Liqueur

1 shot espresso, room temperature

Ice cubes

3 coffee beans for garnish

Milk or heavy cream optional

ESPRESSO ROMANO, ORIGIN UNKNOWN

DESTINATION

Italy, France, United States

TIME

5 minutes

EQUIPMENT

Espresso machine

INGREDIENTS

1 shot espresso

1 lemon

The Espresso Romano is made by rubbing a lemon twist along the rim of an espresso cup. While espresso clearly hails from Italy, the Romano variation is more likely an American or French invention, despite the reference to Rome. Some say it began as a way to clean the glass or a way to cut the bitterness of poorly made espresso. It caught on and is now served in many different countries.

INSTRUCTIONS

Prepare your lemon twist by cutting a ¼ inch lemon slice. Carefully remove the lemon pulp, leaving a ring of lemon rind. Cut across the ring once to create one long strip. Curl the rind tightly, then release. The twist should hold its shape for your garnish. Duplicate the process to create a second lemon strip, but do not twist. Pull a single or double shot of espresso. Rub the white side of the flat lemon strip on the rim of the espresso cup. Use the curled twist for garnish. Sip and enjoy!

FLAT WHITE IN MELBOURNE AND WELLINGTON

There is a spirited debate about which country invented the flat white, so let's celebrate both beautiful places! The flat white is made with espresso and steamed milk. It is served in a smaller glass, which gives it a higher espresso-to-steamed-milk ratio compared to a latte. A flat white typically has microfoam, or less foam than a latte, hence the name flat, as in absent mini mountains of foam. I really love this one!

INSTRUCTIONS

Preheat cup by adding hot water then discarding. Prepare a double shot of espresso in a 6 ounce ceramic mug. Steam approximately 4 ounces of milk and aim to create a small amount of mircofoam. Slowly pour steamed milk into espresso finishing with a thin layer of microfoam on top.

DESTINATION

Australia and New Zealand

TIME

5 minutes

EQUIPMENT

Espresso machine and milk steamer

INGREDIENTS

2 shots espresso

4 ounces milk

FRAPPE IN ATHENS

DESTINATION

Athens, Greece

TIME

5 minutes

EQUIPMENT

Frother or blender

INGREDIENTS

2 tsp instant coffee powder

1 tsp granulated sugar

3 Tbsp cold water

⅔ cup cold water

3 ice cubes

2 Tbsp milk, optional

During the 1957 International Trade Fair in Thessaloniki, a Nestlé employee, Dimitris Vakondios, was on break but couldn't find any hot water to make his Nescafe Classico. He improvised and mixed his instant coffee with cold water in a shaker. It worked! Today the Greek Frappe is served throughout Greece. It's perfect to enjoy outdoors on a beautiful sunny day.

INSTRUCTIONS

Place instant coffee powder, sugar, and 3 tablespoons cold water in a tall glass. Using a handheld frother, process until a thick layer of froth forms. Carefully pour in remaining cold water and ice cubes. Add milk as desired. Serve immediately.

GINGERBREAD LATTE IN THE NORTH POLE

Gingerbread includes a broad category of baked goods typically flavored with ginger, nutmeg, cloves, and cinnamon and sweetened with honey, molasses, or sugar. The earliest evidence of gingerbread was found in ancient ceremonies in Egypt and Greece. Gingerbread shows up later in European history around the 11th century and gingerbread men were eaten by women who hoped it would help them find love. Queen Elizabeth I lavishly treated dignitaries to gingerbread men decorated in their likeness. In the 16th century, Germany created gingerbread houses modeled after the children's tale Hansel and Gretel.

A ubiquitous coffee brand debuted a Gingerbread Latte in 2000 but only serves it today in select international markets. However, you can enjoy this easy recipe inspired by the wildly popular seasonal beverage. The gingerbread house isn't quite as easy but it was so much fun to make!

INSTRUCTIONS

In a saucepan, bring brown sugar, sugar, molasses, cinnamon, and ginger to a boil. Simmer for 5 minutes, stirring often. Remove from heat and stir in vanilla. Meanwhile prepare 2 shots of espresso and prepare steamed milk. Combine 2 tablespoons of the gingerbread syrup with espresso and steamed milk, reserving remaining syrup for another latte tomorrow or a gingerbread cocktail tonight. Top with whipped cream and sprinkled cinnamon.

DESTINATION

North Pole

TIME

15 minutes

EQUIPMENT

Espresso machine

INGREDIENTS

¼ cup brown sugar

½ cup granulated sugar

1 Tbsp molasses

1 tsp cinnamon

½ tsp ginger

1 tsp vanilla

2 shots espresso

¾ cup milk

Homemade whipped cream (optional, see page 28)

Cinnamon for sprinkling

GLARIFFEE IN SONOMA

We're visiting the city of Sonoma, located in the heart of California's wine region. We are attempting to make a recipe so secret it is rumored to be known by only two people and the recipe is stored in a safety deposit box. The glariffee is an abbreviated amalgam combining the words: Glazed Irish Coffee. It was created by the Swiss Hotel in downtown Sonoma. The family hotel proprietors report that their grandfather, Ted Dunlap, co-invented the glariffee with his friend who owned the Buena Vista Cafe (see page 104 for the Buena Vista Irish Coffee recipe).

The secret recipe has never been leaked, so this is a recipe I created in honor of the glariffee, but I am sure I'm missing one of their secret ingredients.

Online comments and reviewers describe the glariffee as "rich and sweet," "potent," "strong and delish," "divine," "like an Irish whiskey but smoother," "cold coffee martini," "out of this world," "cold coffee concoction," and charmingly as a "crazy little Irish coffee."

INSTRUCTIONS

MAKE THE SIMPLE SYRUP

In a small saucepan over medium heat, combine sugar and water. Stir often until sugar is completely dissolved (about 5 minutes). Let cool completely. You'll have leftovers of the simple syrup that can be used in desserts and cocktails.

DESTINATION

Sonoma, California

TIME

10 minutes (and 3 hours to chill the coffee)

EQUIPMENT

Any brewing device

INGREDIENTS

1 cup demerara sugar

½ cup water

4 Tbsp ground coffee (for coffee)

2 Tbsp coffee beans (for coffee-infused whiskey)

2 shots Tullamore Dew whiskey

Homemade whipped cream (see page 28)

INGREDIENTS

1 cup demerara sugar

½ cup water

4 Tbsp ground coffee (for coffee)

2 Tbsp coffee beans (for coffee-infused whiskey)

2 shots Tullamore Dew whiskey

Homemade whipped cream (see page 28)

PREPARE THE GLARIFFEE

Place a shatterproof tall glass in the freezer to chill.

While the glass is chilling, brew two cups of coffee using a French press or your favorite coffee machine. Let cool slightly, then chill for two hours. Meanwhile crush coffee beans using a mortar and pestle or the bottom of a mug or bowl. Soak in Tullamore Dew whiskey for two hours, then strain out coffee beans.

Combine chilled coffee, one or two shots of coffee-infused whiskey, and 4 tablespoons simple syrup. Serve in a chilled glass with homemade whipped cream.

See photo next page.

HORCHATA COLD BREW IN LAGOS

We're going to North Africa for today's coffee trip with stops along the way in Spain and Mexico! We're making an iced cold brew coffee with horchata. Horchata de arroz is one of my favorite flavors from Mexico. It's a cold drink made with rice, cinnamon, and brown sugar. Spain has their own version called an horchata de chufa made by combining ground tiger nuts with milk and sugar. However, the earliest version of this drink began in Nigeria and Mali in 2400 B.C. and is still served today as kuunu aya. Today we are combining an horchata de arroz with a cold brew coffee. It takes 24 hours to make but it's worth the effort. This is one of my favorites of all my coffee trips so far!

INSTRUCTIONS

HORCHATA DE ARROZ

On day one, combine the rice, 1 cup of water, sliced almonds, and cinnamon sticks in a blender. Pulse until coarsely ground. Place mixture in a large bowl and add the remaining water. Cover and place in the refrigerator overnight. On day two, add the milk and brown sugar to the mixture and stir until combined. Strain the mixture through a cheesecloth or fine-mesh sieve into a pitcher for storage. On day one, prepare the coffee concentrate on the following page which also needs to be prepared a day in advance.

DESTINATION

Lagos, Nigeria

TIME

Active 15 minutes; total time 24 hours

EQUIPMENT

Blender, fine-mesh sieve, cheesecloth or paper filter

INGREDIENTS

HORCHATA

1½ cups of uncooked long grain white rice

¼ cup of sliced almonds, toasted

2 cinnamon sticks

3½ cups of lukewarm water

½ cup of brown sugar

2 cups of whole milk or almond milk

½ tsp cinnamon for garnish (optional)

COLD BREW CONCENTRATE

1½ cups coffee beans, coarsely ground

4½ cups of water

COLD BREW CONCENTRATE

Combine the ground coffee beans and water in a large mixing bowl and allow it to sit, covered, overnight. On the next day, use a cheesecloth or similar fabric to line a fine-mesh sieve, then strain the mixture into a large pitcher.

HORCHATA COLD BREW

Add ice to a tall glass. Pour in ½ cup of horchata and ½ cup of cold brew concentrate. Stir to combine and garnish with powdered cinnamon.

See photo on page 97

ICED BLENDED OREO™ COFFEE IN LOS ANGELES

Today we're traveling to Los Angeles to virtually visit my friend Scott Froschauer, an artist who makes playful, creative, and inspiring street sign art. I love his artwork and he is such a good person. We are making the most playful coffee I can think of... an iced, blended Oreo coffee!

INSTRUCTIONS

In a blender, process ice cubes, milk, coffee, and two Oreo cookies until blended to desired consistency. Top with whipped cream and a crushed Oreo.

DESTINATION

Los Angeles, CA

TIME

5 minutes

EQUIPMENT

Any brewing device

INGREDIENTS

½ cup ice cubes

1 cup milk

1 cup brewed coffee, chilled

2 Oreo cookies

1 Oreo cookie, for garnish

Homemade whipped cream (see page 28)

Play Street Sign by Artist Scott Froshauer (scottfroschauer.com)

ICED COFFEE IN KYOTO

DESTINATION

Kyoto, Japan

TIME

5 minutes

EQUIPMENT

Pour over dripper

INGREDIENTS

1 cup ice

10 Tbsp coarsely ground coffee

1½ cups boiling water

This method is an easy and expedient way to enjoy iced coffee. Some say the flavor profile rivals that of a cold brew (see page 71). A Japanese iced coffee is made using a pour over device to brew the coffee directly over ice. We use more coffee and less water while brewing to account for the ice that will quickly melt on contact with the hot water. I experimented with a few different ratios - the following is perfect! It's my new favorite coffee to make!

INSTRUCTIONS

Place ice in the bottom of a Chemex or other similar pour over coffee dripper. Place coffee grounds into filter. Pour 2 tablespoons of nearly boiling water over grounds. Let bloom for 30 seconds. Slowly pour remaining hot water over coffee in a circular motion to evenly saturate grounds. Aim for about a 3 minute brew cycle. Cream and sugar optional.

IRISH COFFEE IN SHANNON

In 1952 the Buena Vista Cafe in San Francisco attempted to replicate the Irish Coffee from the Shannon Airport in Ireland. They finally landed on what they considered to be the right blend and this is that recipe! Homemade whipped cream tops it all off for a perfect holiday weekend brunch at home.

INSTRUCTIONS

Pour hot water into a serving cup to heat glass then discard water. Place sugar cubes in glass. Pour in hot coffee until three-quarters full. Stir until well blended. Add whiskey. Top with whipped cream. Imagine you're in the always crowded Buena Vista Cafe on your way to see the Golden Gate Bridge and hop on a cable car!

DESTINATION

Shannon, Ireland

TIME

5 minutes

EQUIPMENT

Any brewing device

INGREDIENTS

2 sugar cubes

1 cup brewed coffee (Buena Vista uses Oakland's Peerless Coffee & Tea)

1½ oz Irish whiskey (Buena Vista uses Tullamore Dew)

Homemade whipped cream (lightly whipped; stop when very soft peaks form)

JAMAICAN COFFEE IN KINGSTON

DESTINATION

Kingston, Jamaica

TIME

5 minutes

EQUIPMENT

Any brewing device

INGREDIENTS

2 cups brewed coffee (ideally use Blue Mountain coffee beans)

½ shot coffee liqueur (see page 68)

½ shot rum

Homemade whipped cream (see page 28)

Allspice for garnish

Jamaica's coffee farmers produce some of the most sought-after coffee beans in the world. Coffee grown in this rugged mountainous region is certified by the Coffee Industry Board of Jamaica. The Blue Mountains are a UNESCO World Heritage site based on their rich biodiversity and historical significance. The indigenous Tainos fled European colonial slavery by escaping to the Blue Mountains. The Maroons, descendents of African slaves, also escaped to the Blue Mountains where they found everything they needed to survive. They developed a strong spiritual connection with the forest and built a network of trails, hiding places, and refuges to maintain their freedom.

There are many variations of a Jamaican coffee. This recipe includes both coffee liqueur and rum for a perfect spirited blend.

INSTRUCTIONS

Stir together coffee, coffee Liqueur, and rum. Add heaps of whipped cream and sprinkle with allspice. I served my Jamaican coffee with traditional banana fritters. Sip slowly and imagine sitting on a beach with a turquoise ocean just steps away!

Despite the name, allspice is not a blend but rather a single spice made from the dried berries of the Pimenta dioica tree. The dried berries look similar to peppercorns and are native to Jamaica.

KAFFEOST IN NORTHERN SCANDINAVIA

In Sweden, it's called Kaffeost. In Finland, it's Leipäjuusto. Some call it squeaky cheese for the distinctive sound it makes when you bite into it. It originated among the Sami people indigenous to the northern parts of Finland, Sweden, Norway, and Russia. The coffee cheese is served in a wood mug with a handle. This is easier to make than it seems and incredibly tasty.

DESTINATION

Northern Scandinavia

TIME

1 hour 20 minutes

EQUIPMENT

Any brewing device

INSTRUCTIONS

MAKE THE CHEESE

Gently heat raw milk and heavy cream in a large saucepan over low heat. Stir occasionally. Heat to about 98 degrees. Set aside. While you're warming the milk, dissolve rennet in distilled water, which takes 15 minutes. Add dissolved rennet to warm milk as you remove it from heat. Let sit undisturbed for one hour as it curdles. Cut curds into 1 inch pieces if solid or leave as is if already in small pieces. Reheat curds until just before boiling, stirring curds toward center of pot. Remove from heat. Spoon curds into a colander lined with cheesecloth. The curds will be hot, so carefully squeeze whey out of cheese and collect it in a bowl beneath the colander. Fold cheesecloth over curds. Set a heavy weight atop such as a bowl filled with water. Let sit for a few hours or overnight in the fridge until whey has fully separated and cheese is dry. Set in a small baking dish and bake for 20 minutes then broil briefly until golden and dark brown spots appear. That's it - you've made cheese!

INGREDIENTS

4 cups raw milk

¼ cup heavy cream

½ rennet tablet

3 Tbsp distilled water

2 cups black coffee

PREPARE THE COFFEE

Cut cheese into cubes and place a few at the bottom of a wood cup. Brew two cups of coffee using your preferred method. Pour coffee on top of the cheese. Serve with a few pieces of additional cheese on the side.

KAISERMELANGE IN VIENNA

The Kaisermelange is a Viennese speciality. The name translates to "Emperor's Coffee," as the rich and decadent flavors are worthy of an emperor. In the right sunlight, the Kaise Melange also has a golden hue, which also seems fitting for royalty.

INSTRUCTIONS

In a tall glass mug, stir together the egg yolk and honey. Rest a spoon lightly above the yolk layer. In a separate cup, combine espresso and cognac. Slowly pour espresso on top of the yolk layer using the resting spoon to avoid mixing the layers. Heap whipped cream atop the espresso layer. Enjoy the beautiful layers, but stir and combine well before taking your first sip.

DESTINATION

Vienna, Austria

TIME

5 minutes

EQUIPMENT

Espresso machine

INGREDIENTS

1 shot espresso

1 egg yolk (fresh and organic, as it will be consumed raw)

1 Tbsp honey

½ cup homemade whipped cream (see page 28)

1 shot of cognac (optional)

KOPI JAHE IN MEDAN

DESTINATION

Medan, Indonesia

TIME

10 minutes

EQUIPMENT

Saucepan

INGREDIENTS

2 Tbsp coffee, coarsely ground (kopi)

½ inch fresh ginger, smashed (jahe)

2 Tbsp palm sugar

1 cinnamon stick

4 cardamom pods

4 cloves

2 cups water

Kopi Jahe means "coffee with ginger" and the receipe includes an array of warm and aromatic spices. This drink is common throughout Indonesia and was likely influenced by spices arriving from the Middle East. Indonesian stores sell sachets for making Kopi Jahe at home, but it is best made with fresh ingredients.

INSTRUCTIONS

Peel and smash the fresh ginger keeping it whole to easily strain and discard later. Combine all ingredients in a saucepan. Bring to a boil. Reduce to simmer for 8 minutes stirring occasionally. Strain and discard all solid pieces. Serve warm and enjoy!

LATTE IN REYKJAVIK

Iceland imports all their coffee beans, of course, but their roasters are local and legendary. Fun fact: there are no Starbucks® coffee shops in Iceland. Lattes hail from Italy, but are served all over the world and are commonly served in Iceland. As I discovered the coffee preferences in Iceland, I also discovered Iceland's traditional Hjó nabandsæla, translated as a happy marriage cake.

If I owned a coffee shop this would be the only dessert I'd serve. It's as delicious as Iceland is beautiful!

INSTRUCTIONS

Prepare a double shot of espresso in a large latte mug. Steam or froth milk in a separate small pitcher then pour over espresso.

DESTINATION
Reykjavik, Iceland

TIME
5 minutes

EQUIPMENT
Espresso machine

INGREDIENTS
2 shots espresso

1 cup whole milk (or oat milk)

MAPLE WHIPPED CREAM COFFEE IN QUEBEC CITY

DESTINATION

Quebec City, Canada

TIME

10 minutes

EQUIPMENT

Any coffee brewer

INGREDIENTS

1 cup of coffee

½ cup homemade whipped cream (see page 28)

1 tsp maple syrup

Maple syrup for garnish

According to the Coffee Association of Canada, espresso-based drinks are gaining in popularity, but Canadians still overwhelming prefer a standard cup of coffee. I like the simplicity, but I couldn't resist adding a touch of maple whipped cream, too!

INSTRUCTIONS

Prepare whipped cream then add maple syrup. Stir to combine. Prepare one cup of coffee using your favorite brew method. Heap whipped cream atop coffee. Drizzle with maple syrup as desired.

MAZAGRAN IN MAZAGRAN

The Mazagran, named for the Algerian city where it originated, is a cold, sweetened coffee. Some say this is where iced coffee first began. In 1837, France invaded Algeria. At one point, one hundred French soldiers were captured. During their detainment, with very little resources, the prisoners cut their coffee with cold water, rather than their typical brandy. The taste caught on and soon grew in popularity. The Portuguese built on this method by adding lemon. Imagine a coffee version of an Arnold Palmer.

INSTRUCTIONS

Using a French press, brew one cup of strong coffee. Add sugar to coffee and stir until dissolved. Fill a tall, heat-resistant glass with ice, then pour hot coffee over ice. You will want to use freshly brewed hot coffee, as it melts the ice cubes just enough to add the right balance of coffee and water. Stir in lemon juice and serve immediately.

DESTINATION

Mazagran, Algeria

TIME

10 minutes

EQUIPMENT

French press

INGREDIENTS

Ice cubes

1 cup strong coffee

2 Tbsp freshly squeezed lemon juice

2 Tbsp granulated sugar

1 lemon wedge or wheel (optional)

MOCHA FRAPPUCCINO IN BOSTON

Did you know this dreamy frozen coffee was invented by Coffee Connection, an Eastern Massachusetts coffee chain, in 1992? The founder, George Howell, was inspired by the Cappuccino Granita–a frozen Italian dessert. Two years later a very well known coffee chain bought the coffeeshop chain and added the Frappuccino to their global menu.

INSTRUCTIONS

In a blender, combine ice cubes, chilled espresso, milk, chocolate syrup, sugar, and xanthan gum or pudding mix. Blend until thick and smooth but do not over blend. The secret ingredient will make the Frappuccino extra smooth and will prevent separation. Pour into a tall chilled glass or mason jar. Top with homemade whipped cream and heaps of chocolate syrup.

DESTINATION

Boston, Massachusetts

TIME

5 minutes prep;
1 hour wait time

EQUIPMENT

Espresso machine and blender

INGREDIENTS

1 cup ice cubes

2 shots espresso, chilled completely

1/3 cup milk

2 Tbsp chocolate syrup and extra for topping

1 Tbsp sugar

Secret ingredient:
1/4 tsp xanthan gum or 1 tsp dry instant vanilla pudding mix

Homemade whipped cream (see page 28)

MOCHA LATTE HOT CHOCOLATE BOMB IN BOISE

This coffee is as delicious as it is dramatic! A latte is transformed into a mocha with the addition of a decadent chocolate bomb. Upon melting, the chocolate bomb releases mocha and marshmallows. The chocolate bomb was invented in Boise, Idaho, in 2019 and quickly went viral on social media.

INSTRUCTIONS

MAKE THE CHOCOLATE BOMBS

Using a sharp knife, finely chop your chocolate into small pieces.

Place chocolate into a microwave-safe bowl and heat for 30 seconds.

Stir the chocolate, then heat again for 15 seconds.

Stir again and continue to heat at 15 second intervals until the chocolate is almost melted but not fully melted. Do not heat for longer intervals, nor heat above 90 degrees.

Using a paintbrush, paint a thin layer of chocolate into the molds and refrigerate for 5 minutes.

Paint a second coat of chocolate over the first. Be sure to paint chocolate all the way to the rim to make a perfect half sphere. Refrigerate again for 5 minutes.

DESTINATION
Boise, Idaho

TIME
1 hour

EQUIPMENT
candy thermometer, silicon 2½ inch sphere molds, paint brush

INGREDIENTS

CHOCOLATE BOMBS
SERVES 6

12 ounces high quality semisweet chocolate

3 packets hot cocoa mix

1 cup mini marshmallows

LATTE

2 shots espresso

1 cup steamed milk (see page 26)

Remove from refrigerator. Add 1 tablespoon of hot cocoa mix and as many marshmallows as will fit into the half spheres. Gently remove half spheres from molds and set aside on wax paper.

Heat a small baking sheet in the oven. Remove from oven. Working quickly and carefully, place the empty halfsphere lightly onto warm baking sheet to slightly melt the rim. Immediately and gently press the empty half atop the cocoa-filled bottom half. Press gently to seal. If needed, paint a layer of chocolate around the seam. Place in refrigerator for 5 minutes.

Melt white chocolate using the same microwave method above. Using a frosting piping bag or a ziplock with a clipped corner, drizzle white chocolate across the chocolate bombs as decoration. Place in refrigerator for 5 minutes to set.

PREPARE THE LATTE

Prepare espresso in a large latte mug. Add steamed milk. Add one chocolate bomb and watch as it dramaticllay bursts to reveal mocha and marshmallows. Gently stir and enjoy!

See photo next page.

MOROCCAN COFFEE IN MARRAKESH

DESTINATION

Marrakesh, Morocco

TIME

10 minutes

EQUIPMENT

French press

INGREDIENTS

3 Tbsp coffee beans

¼ tsp ground cardamom (or seeds from 4 cardamom pods)

¼ tsp whole cloves

¼ tsp freshly grated nutmeg

¼ tsp ground cinnamon

⅛ tsp ground ginger

⅛ tsp freshly cracked black pepper

A dash of salt

1 sugar cube (optional)

While many associate mint tea with Morocco, this North African country also has a rich coffee culture. A traditional Moroccan coffee is reminiscent of the Kopi Jahe we made from Indonesia (see page 113), but with the addition of nutmeg and black pepper. The blend is fragrant and uplifting.

INSTRUCTIONS

In a coffee grinder, process coffee and spices until coarsely ground. Preheat your French press by adding hot water, swirling, then discarding water. Place ground coffee and spice mixture into coffee press. Boil water; remove from heat and let sit for 30 seconds. This will bring your water to the recommended temperature of 195 - 205 degrees Fahrenheit. Pour hot water into fresh press. Stir once to ensure grounds are properly immersed in water. Add lid but do not depress plunger. Let steep for 4 minutes. Slowly lower the plunger. Pour into a mug and add sugar to taste.

OLIANG IN BANGKOK

This popular Thai iced coffee is served throughout Thailand and especially at roadside stands. You can make it with store-bought powder, but we're making it from scratch. There are many variations but most have soybeans, dried corn, sesame seeds, coffee, and a sweetener. I've never made anything with soybeans before and this is delicious! It tastes like a toasted coffee, rather than a roasted coffee.

INSTRUCTIONS

In a large, dry frying pan over medium heat, toast soybeans and dried corn until golden brown (about 5 minutes). Remove from heat. Stir white sesame seeds into the soybeans and corn. Let cool completely then add coffee beans. Using a grinder or mortar and pestle, grind into a coarse mixture. In a medium saucepan, bring water to a boil. Remove from heat and add the coarsely ground coffee and soybean/corn mixture. Cover and let steep for 5 minutes. Strain the liquid using muslin or a coffee filter. Stir in sugar. Add ice cubes and the sweetened condensed milk, then serve immediately.

DESTINATION
Bangkok, Thailand

TIME
10 minutes

EQUIPMENT
Frying pan, saucepan, coffee grinder, muslin or paper filter

INGREDIENTS
2 Tbsp soybeans

2 Tbsp dried corn

1 Tbsp white sesame seeds

4 Tbsp coffee beans

2 cups water

1 Tbsp sugar (white or brown)

2 ice cubes

1 Tbsp sweetened condensed milk (optional)

PEPPERMINT MOCHA LATTE IN THE NORTH POLE

DESTINATION

North Pole

TIME

10 minutes

EQUIPMENT

Espresso machine

INGREDIENTS

1 cup sugar

1 cup water

1 bunch fresh mint leaves

3 Tbsp chocolate chips (milk chocolate or dark)

¾ cup milk

1 double shot espresso

1 small crushed candy cane

Homemade whipped cream (see page 28)

Technically the Peppermint Mocha Latte was invented in Seattle in 2000 by a ubiquitous coffee brand, but this delicious treat has a holiday spirit that clearly hails from the North Pole. This is a decadent copycat recipe of a latte that has now become a familiar seasonal special in coffee shops around the world.

INSTRUCTIONS

MAKE THE PEPPERMINT SIMPLE SYRUP

In a small saucepan over medium heat, stir water and sugar until sugar is completely dissolved (about 4 minutes). Reduce heat to low and add fresh mint leaves; steep for 15 minutes. You'll have plenty of leftover peppermint simple syrup that will last 1 month in a mason jar or airtight container in the refrigerator. Incorporate peppermint syrup in your favorite desserts or holiday cocktails.

PREPARE THE PEPPERMINT MOCHA

In a small saucepan over medium heat, melt chocolate chips with milk. Stir often. Meanwhile pull a double shot espresso in a regular sized coffee mug. Add melted chocolate milk and peppermint simple syrup to espresso. Top with homemade whipped cream and crushed candy canes.

POUR OVER COFFEE IN STRATFORD-UPON-AVON

We're making a simple brewed coffee with milk to serve alongside a traditional British coffee cake. Interestingly, American coffee cakes are served with coffee but don't actually have any coffee in them. The British Coffee and Walnut Cake has coffee within the cake itself and also in the rich buttercream frosting. It's delicious, especially the coffee frosting.

Coffee gained popularity in Britain just after Shakespeare graced us with his 37 plays, so you won't find any references to coffee in his writings. Shakespeare was born in the small market town of Stratford-upon-Avon, which now boasts dozens of coffee shops.

INSTRUCTIONS

Heat water in a teapot or saucepan until boiling. Set aside for 30 seconds to bring the water to the recommended temperature. Using your favorite pour over device such as a Chemex, slowly pour water over coffee grounds until just barely covered. Let sit for 30 seconds allowing coffee to bloom. Slowly pour remaining hot water over coffee grounds. Serve immediately in a British tea cup with milk.

DESTINATION
Stratford-upon-Avon, England

TIME
5 minutes

EQUIPMENT
Pour over device

INGREDIENTS
1 cup water

1 heaping tablespoon coffee (fine to medium grind)

1 Tbsp milk (optional)

PUMPKIN SPICE LATTE IN SEATTLE

DESTINATION

Seattle, Washington

TIME

10 minutes

EQUIPMENT

Espresso machine

INGREDIENTS

2 cups milk

3 Tbsp pumpkin purée

2 Tbsp granulated sugar

2 tsp pumpkin pie spice (or prepare your own using 2 parts cinnamon, 1 part nutmeg, 1 part ground ginger, ½ part ground cloves)

1 tsp vanilla

The pumpkin spice latte was invented by an executive who led the espresso team at a ubiquitous coffee chain in Seattle in 2003 and was inspired by America's seasonal love of pumpkin pie. The pumpkin is native to North America and was likely served as a vegetable side dish at the first Thanksgiving in 1621. However, pumpkin pie originated in England in the 17th century and eventually made its way into American cookbooks by 1796. This version of a pumpkin spice latte is seriously jaw-droppingly delicious!

INSTRUCTIONS

In a small pot over medium heat, warm milk, pumpkin purée, and sugar until just below boiling. Remove from heat and add pumpkin pie spice and vanilla. Meanwhile pull a single or double shot into a regular-sized coffee mug. Pour half of the pumpkin milk mixture into your mug. Save the remaining half in the refrigerator for a latte the next day, or combine with another espresso shot for a second serving. Top with homemade whipped cream (page 28) and sprinkled pumpkin pie spice.

RAKTAJINO ON PLANET KRONOS

Is there coffee in the cosmos? Just as coffee unites us on Earth, we find evidence that other galaxies share our love of coffee. In Star Trek, Klingons enjoy their Raktajino, a coffee served steamed or iced. Without a Star Trek replicator, I am improvising to make this iced version.

INSTRUCTIONS

Make 5 shots of espresso. Add coffee ice cream. Sprinkle with cayenne pepper. Exclaim yISop! which means bon appétit in Klingon.

DESTINATION

Planet Kronos of the Star Klingon

TIME

5 minutes

EQUIPMENT

Replicator or an espresso machine

INGREDIENTS

5 shots espresso

½ cup coffee ice cream

Cayenne pepper for garnish

RICE COFFEE IN THE WESTERN VISAYAS

DESTINATION

Western Visayas, Philippines

TIME

35 minutes

EQUIPMENT

Frying Pan

INGREDIENTS

½ cup uncooked white rice

1 cup water

We're going to make a coffee without any coffee beans! We're making "Rice Coffee," which is made in the provinces of the Philippines. Simply roast uncooked rice in a frying pan until dark brown, nearly black. It's really good! It reminded me more of a strong tea than a coffee, and presented a nice, rich, toasted flavor.

I'm serving this alongside Bibingka - a traditional Filipino dessert baked in banana leaves and topped with queso de bola, coconut, and salted eggs. It's often served with coffee. With my Filipino heritage, this dessert and coffee combo is one of my favorites.

INSTRUCTIONS

In a dry frying pan over medium-high heat, roast uncooked rice. Stir frequently and keep a close eye as rice can burn easily. You'll want to have good ventilation, as roasting rice will create a bit of smoke. Roast until very dark brown, nearly black. Remove from heat. Using a mortar and pestle, coarsely grind the roasted rice. Combine 2 tablespoons roasted rice with 1 cup boiling water. You'll have extra rice left over for a second cup of rice coffee. Let steep for 5 minutes and enjoy!

RISTRETTO, ESPRESSO, AND LUNGO IN ROME

As we explore coffees from around the world, it's no surprise that we keep coming back to Italy. We're having a taste test comparing a ristretto, an espresso, and a lungo. A single shot of espresso is about 25 ml. A ristretto is made the same way but we restrict the water by only pulling 15 ml, which intensifies the flavor and avoids a bit of the bitterness. A lungo uses 50 ml of water, which creates a more mild and thin espresso but has more bitter notes. There are volumes written about the flavor complexities of each method, so enjoy experimenting with each. I think there is a reason the standard espresso is the most well-known method - it definitely won in my taste test.

DESTINATION

Rome, Italy

TIME

5 minutes

EQUIPMENT

Espresso machine

INSTRUCTIONS

Given the variances between espresso machines, please refer to your instruction manual for more specific details and guidance.

ESPRESSO

Pull a normal shot of espresso from your manual espresso machine using approximately 25 ml of water.

RISTRETTO

Use the same amount of ground espresso, but restrict the water flow using approximately 15 ml of water.

INGREDIENTS

90 ml water

21 grams ground coffee for espresso (7 grams per shot)

LUNGO

Use the same amount of ground espresso, but increase the water flow using approximately 50 ml of water.

The recommendation for a proper tasting is to try a sip immediately after brewing. Stir to incorporate the crema for your second sip. Then finish the rest in your final sip(s). You'll notice three distinct flavor profiles with each sip.

SEA SALTED ICED COFFEE IN TAIPEI

DESTINATION

Taipei, Taiwan

TIME

10 minutes

EQUIPMENT

Any coffee brewer; hand mixer

INGREDIENTS

1 cup cold brew coffee (see page 71)

1 Tbsp simple syrup (see page 94)

½ cup whipped cream (see page 28)

¼ tsp sea salt (preferably Maldon)

Cocoa powder or cinnamon for garnish

The Sea Salted Iced Coffee was made famous by a popular bakery based in Taiwan with locations around the world. The sweetened iced coffee is topped with a sea salted whipped cream. On its own sea salt whipped cream isn't that pleasant, but mixed in with the bold coffee it adds a lovely sweet and salty complement.

INSTRUCTIONS

Fill cup with ice. Add cold brew coffee and simple syrup. Stir to combine. In a small bowl, stir together whipped cream with sea salt until just combined. Heap whipped cream atop iced coffee. Sprinkle with cocoa powder or cinnamon.

S'MORES LATTE IN EVERYTOWN, USA

The S'more makes its first official appearance in a Girl Scout guidebook in 1927 called "Tramping and Trailing with the Girl Scouts." Commercial products Mallomars (1913) and MoonPies (1917) predate the S'more and had similar ingredients, but it is the roasted marshmallow from a real campfire that makes the S'more such a memorable taste. The primary ingredients are beautifully blended in this latte and adorned with an optional and over-the-top garnish of two full size S'mores.

DESTINATION

Everytown, USA

TIME

20 minutes

EQUIPMENT

Sauce pan, Espresso machine

INGREDIENTS

½ cup sugar

½ cup water

4 large marshmallows

1 tsp vanilla extract

2 shots espresso

1 Tbsp chocolate syrup

½ cup steamed milk or milk alternative

whipped cream (see page 28)

OPTIONAL BUT RECOMMENDED GARNISH

1 wooden stick (8 inches)

2 graham cracker squares

2 large marshmallows

1 Hershey's™ chocolate bar

INSTRUCTIONS

MAKE THE MARSHMALLOW SYRUP

In a saucepan over medium heat, stir together sugar and water until sugar is dissolved. Meanwhile toast 4 large marshmallows over an open flame on stove or in broiler until golden brown and slightly charred. Stir marshmallows into saucepan with sugar and water until marshmallows are dissolved. Remove from heat. Add vanilla. Let cool.

PREPARE THE LATTE

Combine two shots espresso, fresh marshmallow syrup, chocolate syrup, and steamed milk. Top with whipped cream. Ridiculous, over-the-top two-tiered S'mores garnish is optional but recommended!

MAKE A S'MORES GARNISH

Place one small drop of water in the middle of the graham cracker square. Use a wooden stick (preferably with a pointed end) and slowly twist the skewer into the graham cracker in the spot that is slightly soft from the waterdrop. Remove wooden stick and set aside. Repeat on second graham cracker square. Warm the tip of a skewer over an open flame and use it to to create a similar hole in the chocolate square. Set aside. Place marshmallows on fire-proof skewers. Carefully hold marshmallow over an open flame until golden brown or charred if you prefer. Place the ingredients onto the wooden stick using the pre-defined holes and in the following order: graham cracker, chocolate square, marshmallow, graham cracker, then repeat.

STRONG COFFEE FIKA IN STOCKHOLM

One of the most endearing and lovely traditions in Swedish culture is the fika. You might translate fika as a coffee break, but it signifies much more than that. A fika is a time to enjoy coffee and a sweet pastry, but it's more about socializing. I love how it creates a pause in the day to connect with others - it feels both cozy and grounded. The word fika can be used as both a noun and a verb. "Let's fika at home today" or "I can't wait to enjoy a fika in Sweden again!"

While Swedes enjoy all types of coffee, the most common is an extremely strong black coffee. That's what we'll have today along with a homemade kanelbullar (Swedish cinnamon bun).

INSTRUCTIONS

Preheat French press by adding hot water, swirling, then discarding water. Boil hot water, remove from heat and set aside for 30 seconds. This will bring your water to the recommended temperature of 195 to 205 degrees Fahrenheit. Pour just enough hot water into French press to cover the grounds. Stir once to ensure grounds are properly immersed in water. Let sit for 30 seconds allowing coffee to bloom. Add remaining hot water. Add lid but do not depress plunger. Let steep for exactly 4 minutes. Slowly lower the plunger. Pour into your favorite cozy mug, call a friend, and enjoy your fika!

> *Pair your strong coffee with a traditional Swedish Kanelbullar (cinnamon bun) and enjoy the hygge, the Danish and Norwegian term for coziness or the art of enjoying life's quiet and simple pleasures!*

DESTINATION

Stockholm, Sweden

TIME

5 minutes

EQUIPMENT

French press

INGREDIENTS

3 Tbsp ground coffee

1 cup water

TINTO IN BOGOTÁ

Colombia is the world's third largest coffee exporter. The high-quality beans are made possible thanks to Colombia's unique climate, abundant rainfall, and nutrient-rich soil. There are an estimated 600,000 coffee farmers in Colombia. The most popular coffee is a Tinto, a small black coffee that is prepared in an olleta, a traditional iron pitcher.

Pair your coffee with a Colombian traditional dessert, Esponjado de Café, which is a decadent coffee-infused mousse.

INSTRUCTIONS

Bring water to a gentle rolling boil in an olleta or use a standard saucepan. If you prefer a sweetener, add the optional panela now and stir occasionally until sugar is fully dissolved. Remove pot from heat. Add coffee grounds and let steep for four minutes. After the grounds settle at the bottom of the pot, slowly pour coffee into a mug and attempt to keep the coffee grounds at the bottom of the pot.

DESTINATION

Bogotá, Colombia

TIME

5 minutes

EQUIPMENT

Olleta (iron pitcher) or a saucepan

INGREDIENTS

2 cups water

1 Tbsp panela (unrefined whole cane sugar, optional)

2 Tbsp coffee, coarsely ground

The coffee producers in Colombia are making significant progress towards more sustainable and wildlife-friendly farming practices. Learn more on page 14.

TURKISH COFFEE IN ISTANBUL AND TBILISI

Turkish Coffee clearly hails from Turkey, but neighboring countries, such as Georgia, also have a long tradition of drinking Turkish Coffee. The stovetop version is made by boiling coffee grounds twice and adding sugar. I'm pairing this with khachapuri, a delicious cheese-filled and egg-topped bread featured in Georgian cuisine.

INSTRUCTIONS

Add water and sugar, if desired, to a saucepan over medium heat; stir gently a few times. Drop in coffee grounds but do not stir. Let the coffee grounds float on the surface. Watch the saucepan carefully. Over medium high heat, bring to just below boiling. If the pot begins to boil, immediately remove from heat. As foam begins to form, gently remove foam with a spoon and place foam in your demitasse serving cup. Remove coffee from heat to ensure water does not boil, then return saucepan to medium heat. As foam forms again, slowly pour into demitasse cup and try not to disturb the foam. The more foam, the more delicious the coffee!

> **Georgia is the birthplace of wine. When arriving in Tbilisi, the immigration officers welcome every visitor with a small bottle of wine (pictured here).**

DESTINATION
Istanbul, Turkey and Tbilisi, Georgia

TIME
10 minutes

EQUIPMENT
An ibrik (a traditional copper Turkish coffee pot) or a saucepan

INGREDIENTS
1 cup water

1 Tbsp finely ground coffee

1 tsp granulated sugar (optional during brew process)

VIETNAMESE ICED COFFEE IN HANOI

DESTINATION

Hanoi, Vietnam

TIME

5 minutes

EQUIPMENT

Any coffee brewer

INGREDIENTS

2 cups brewed coffee, cooled to room temperature

2 to 4 Tbsp sweetened condensed milk

To make a traditional Vietnamese Iced Coffee, you'll need a metal phin filter, which is commonly used to brew coffee in Vietnam. But you can still make a delicious version using your favorite brew method. I prefer to make a strong coffee using a French press.

Did you know that Vietnam is the second largest producer of coffee beans?

INSTRUCTIONS

Brew a strong cup of coffee using your favorite brewing device. Let cool to room temperature. Fill a tall cup with ice. Add coffee and sweetened condensed milk. Stir well and enjoy this delectable coffee!

WHITE RUSSIAN IN MOSCOW

While the origin is hazy, the White Russian is said to have been invented in Brussels by a bartender at the Hotel Metropole in 1949. Sixteen years later, the recipe made its first appearance in print in the Oakland Tribune. The Russian reference is simply in recognition of using a good Russian vodka as the base. The popularity of the White Russian skyrocketed when The Dude made it his cocktail of choice in The Big Lebowski, a film that takes place in Los Angeles.

INSTRUCTIONS

Fill your cocktail glass with ice. Add and stir vodka and coffee liqueur. Slowly add heavy cream and watch the distinctive swirls appears as the contrasting colors combine.

DESTINATION

Moscow, Russia

TIME

5 minutes; 48 hours if making homemade coffee liqueur

EQUIPMENT

None

INGREDIENTS

3 oz vodka (approx ⅓ cup)

⅓ cup heavy cream

⅓ cup coffee liqueur (see page 68)

WORLD'S BEST CUP OF COFFEE IN NEW YORK CITY

The 2003 Christmas movie Elf is one of my favorite comedies of all time. In one of the many charming scenes, Buddy the Elf stumbles across a New York coffee shop window with a sign for the "World's Best Cup of Coffee." Buddy the Elf, in his delightful naivety, marches into the coffee shop and congratulates the staff on their achievement.

In a later scene, Buddy the Elf makes a ridiculous sugar-laden spaghetti breakfast with some of his favorite treats including Pop Tarts, chocolate syrup, marshmallows, and sprinkles. I don't recommend it, but I couldn't resist recreating the Elf's version of the "World's Best Cup of Coffee" in a book about global coffee recipes.

INSTRUCTIONS

Brew coffee using a diner-style machine that hasn't been properly cleaned in several years. Let sit on warming plate for at least five hours to truly achieve that familiar taste only available at your favorite local diner.

> **There are a whopping five coffee scenes In Elf! 1) Buddy the Elf discovers the "world's best cup of coffee" 2) Buddy's dad turns down Buddy's spaghetti breakfast and opts for coffee instead 3) Buddy tastes coffee at his dad's office (he doesn't like it!) 4) Buddy's mailroom friend shares his "syrup" (aka whiskey) with Buddy to pour into his coffee 5) Buddy surprises Jovie with the world's best cup of coffee.**

DESTINATION
New York, New York

TIME
10 minutes

EQUIPMENT
Any coffee brewer

INGREDIENTS
8 cups water

1 packet ground coffee for restaurant coffee machines (2 ½ ounces ground coffee from an unrecognizable brand)

BONUS RECIPE

BUDDY THE ELF'S SPAGHETTI BREAKFAST

INGREDIENTS

2 cups cooked spaghetti

¼ cup small marshmallows

¼ cup M&M's

1 chocolate or S'mores Pop Tart

1 Tbsp chocolate syrup

1 Tbsp caramel syrup

Cook 2 cups spaghetti according to package instructions. Add marshmallows, M&Ms, crumbled Pop Tart, and syrups. Just like Buddy the Elf, eat with your hands and sing Christmas carols.

YUANYANG IN HONG KONG

DESTINATION

Hong Kong

TIME

10 minutes

EQUIPMENT

Any coffee brewer

INGREDIENTS

1 cup water

2 tsp Ceylon loose black tea leaves (or tea bag)

2 Tbsp sweetened condensed milk

¾ cup hot brewed coffee

Yuanyang (also known as yuenyeung) is a combination of tea and coffee that originated in Hong Kong. In English, yuanyang translates to mandarin duck. According to legend, this popular drink was named after the mandarin duck because they mate for life, signifying that coffee and tea are meant to be together. While it may sound like an unexpected combination, the flavors blend well and offer a refreshing new twist on two traditional tastes.

INSTRUCTIONS

Boil water then pour over tea leaves. Cover and steep for four minutes. If using loose tea leaves, strain the tea and discard leaves. Stir in sweetened condensed milk. Combine with cup hot coffee.

Iced Yuanyang is also delightful. Simply let cool then serve over ice. For a lighter, less sweet version, use evaporated milk instead of sweetened condensed milk.

ACKNOWLEDGMENTS

It's been a long and fulfilling journey to learn how to turn a simple coffee bean into my favorite affogato. Sixty recipes and thousands of photos later, I'm thankful to everyone who supported the creation of this cookbook.

Family and Friends:

I am immensely grateful to my family and friends for their enthusiastic support as I shared my coffee adventures on Instagram. It was thanks to your likes, comments, and encouragement that this book exists today. Special thanks to Michael Duncan (who sparked my love of travel, food, and coffee!), Mike Conroy, Haidee Conroy, Heather George, Kim Rogers, Liberty Unrath, Linda Warren, Sylvia Stephenson, Stephen Ham, Megan Miller, Suzy Smith, Sam Goldman, Mary Denys Brandão, Melitas Minas, the Sham and Averia family, Emily Yam, Roger Wu, Danny Koch, Mia Quagliarello, Laura Frey, Yury Rozenbaum, Darian Shapiro, David Katz, Angel Vargas, Juan Castano, Pascal Radaoui, Amy Toyama, Frederick Smith, Ashley-Lane Roberts, Henry Dos Santos, Meghan Cosgrove, Marisela Cortez-Hernandez, Desiree Dlugosz, Scott Froschauer, Marat Oyvetsky, Meg Hilletework-Tesfaye, Will Chase, Jeffrey Berke, Katie Hazard, Iris Ronly, Justin McGhee, and Devon Cichoski.

Cookbook Designer:

A heartfelt thanks to Christine Foltzer whose creative touch has elevated the visual charm of this cookbook. Your ability to turn text and photography into beautiful designs has truly made this project a joy to create. Thank you for your collaboration and talent.

Cookbook Editor:
Thank you to Claire Atkinson who improved the writing and clarity of each recipe. Your attention to detail and love of coffee made all the difference.

Eco-friendly Coffee and Conservation Team:
Special thanks to Dr. Mauricio Vela-Vargas, Luisa Rincon-Bustamante, Maria Camila Villegas, Germán Forero-Medina for your inspiring work to save the Andean bear. Additional thanks to Todd Stevens, the Forest Frontiers team, and our global team of dedicated scientists, conservationists, and supporters of Wildlife Conservation Society for protecting wildlife and wild places around the world.

Coffee Farmers and Producers:
To the hardworking farmers and local producers who provide the world with the finest coffee beans, thank you for your commitment to quality and sustainability.

Book Authors:
Coffee and books are two of my favorite treasures. While photographing each coffee, I often pulled books from my shelves to feature alongside the coffee. Thank you to the many authors whose books add color and meaning to these pages.

Readers and Coffee Enthusiasts:
To the readers and coffee enthusiasts who embark on this journey—you are my people. May these coffee recipes bring you joy and delight!

Happy brewing!

INDEX

RECIPES THAT REQUIRE AN ESPRESSO MACHINE

Affogato in Florence 32
Café con Miel in Valencia 44
Café Cubano in Havana 47
Cafe Hafuch in Tel Aviv 51
Caffè Americano in the USA 40
Cappuccino in Milan 55
Charcoal Coffee in Cairo 56
Coffee Lassi in Mumbai 67
Cortado in Basque Country 72
Einspänner in Vienna 79
Espresso in Milan 83
Espresso Martini in Sydney 84
Espresso Romano, Origin Unknown 87
Flat White in Melbourne and Wellington 88
Gingerbread Latte in the North Pole 92
Kaisermelange in Vienna 110
Latte in Reykjavik 114
Mocha Frappuccino in Boston 121
Mocha Latte Hot Chocolate Bomb in Boise 122
Peppermint Mocha Latte in the North Pole 131
Pumpkin Spice Latte in Seattle 135
Raktajino on Planet Kronos 136
Ristretto, Espresso, and Lungo in Rome 140
S'mores Latte in Everytown, USA 144

RECIPES THAT REQUIRE ANY COFFEE BREWER

Airplane Coffee 35
Bulletproof Coffee in Silicon Valley 39
Café Au Lait in Paris 43
Café Mocha in Mokha 52
Coconut Milk Coffee in Kona 60
Coffee and Cola Float in Rio de Janeiro 63
Coffee Jelly in Batangas 64
Eggnog Latte in London 76
Es Alpukat in Jakarta 80
Glariffee in Sonoma 94
Iced Blended Oreo™ Coffee in Los Angeles 100
Iced Coffee in Kyoto 103
Irish Coffee in Shannon 104
Jamaican Coffee in Kingston 107
Kaffeost in Northern Scandinavia 108
Maple Whipped Cream Coffee in Quebec City 117
Mazagran in Mazagran 118
Moroccan Coffee in Marrakesh 127
Pour Over Coffee in Stratford-upon-Avon 132
Sea Salted Iced Coffee in Taipei 143
Strong Coffee Fika in Stockholm 146
Vietnamese Iced Coffee in Hanoi 153
World's Best Cup of Coffee in New York City 156
Yuanyang in Hong Kong 159

RECIPES THAT REQUIRE STANDARD KITCHEN TOOLS (NO SPECIAL COFFEE EQUIPMENT)

Arabic Coffee in Abu Dhabi 36

Café de Olla in Mexico City 48

Chicory Café Au Lait in New Orleans 59

Coffee Liqueur in Veracruz 68

Cold Brew in Tokyo 71

Dalgona Coffee in Seoul 75

Frappe in Athens 91

Horchata Cold Brew in Lagos 98

Kopi Jahe in Medan 113

Oliang in Bangkok 128

Rice Coffee in the Western Visayas 139

Tinto in Bogotá 149

Turkish Coffee in Istanbul and Tbilisi 150

White Russian in Moscow 154

INDEX

RECIPES BY COUNTRY

Algeria 118
Australia 84, 88
Austria 79, 110
Basque Country 72
Brazil 63
Canada 117
Colombia 149
Cuba 47
Egypt 56
England 76, 132
France 43
Georgia 150
Greece 91
Hong Kong 159
Iceland 114
India 67
Indonesia 80, 113
Ireland 104
Israel 51
Italy 32, 55, 83, 140
Jamaica 107
Japan 71, 103
Mexico 48, 68
Morocco 127
New Zealand 88
Nigeria 98
Other 35, 87, 92, 131, 136
Philippines 64, 139

Russia 154
Scandinavia 108
South Korea 75
Spain 44
Sweden 146
Taiwan 143
Thailand 128
Turkey 150
United Arab Emirates 36
United States 39, 40, 59, 60, 94, 100, 121, 122, 135, 144, 156
Vietnam 153
Yemen 52

DESTINATION COFFEE PHOTOGRAPHY INCLUDES THE FOLLOWING BOOKS. LISTED ALPHABETICALLY BY AUTHOR'S LAST NAME.

Al Aswany, Alaa. *The Yacoubian Building.* Translated by Humphrey Davies. The American University in Cairo Press, 2005.

Amirejib, Chabua. *Data Tutashkhia*. 1973. Herald of Georgia, 2019.

Brin, David. *The Transparent Society: Will Technology Force Us To Choose Between Privacy And Freedom? Basic* Books, 1999.

Brockman, John. *This Will Make You Smarter: New Scientific Concepts to Improve Your Thinking.* Harper Perennial, 2012.

Casey, Susan. *The Wave: In Pursuit of the Rogues, Freaks, and Giants of the Ocean.* Anchor, 2011.

Chomsky, Noam. *Rogue States: The Rule of Force in World Affairs*. 2000. Haymarket Books, 2015.

Dangarembga, Tsitsi. *Nervous Conditions*. 1998. Seal Press, 1996.

Davis, Angela Y. *Freedom is a Constant Struggle: Ferguson, Palestine, and the Foundations of a Movement.* Haymarket Books, 2016.

de Beauvoir, Simone. *Le Deuxieme Sexe*. 1949. Gallimard Education, 1986.

DiAngelo, Robin. *White Fragility: Why It's So Hard for White People to Talk About Racism.* Beacon Press, 2018.

Doidge, Norman. *The Brain That Changes Itself: Stories of Personal Triumph from the Frontiers of Brain Science.* Penguin Life, 2007.

Domenici, Davide. *Mexico: A Guide to the Archaeological Sites.* White Star Editions, 2001.

Dunwell, Steve. *Extraordinary Boston.* Back Bay Press, 1994.

Earle, Sylvia A. *Sea Change: A Message of the Oceans.* Ballantine Books, 1996.

Enloe, Cynthia. *Bananas, Beaches and Bases: Making Feminist Sense of International Politics.* University of California Press, 1990.

Fodor's Essential Australia. Fodor's, 2016.

Four Huts: Asian Writings on the Simple Life. Translated by Burton Watson. Shambhala, 2002.

Frankopan, Peter. *Les Nouvelles Routes de la Soie.* Bloomsbury, 2018.

Garcia Lorca, Federico. *Yerma: Poema tragico en tres actos y seis cuardos*. 1934. Ediciones Catedra, S A, 1990.

García Márquez, Gabriel. *El amor en los tiempos del cólera*. 1985. Vintage Espanol, 2007.

Gethin, Rupert. *The Foundations of Buddhism*. Oxford University Press, 1998.

Gombrich, E. H. *A Little History of the World*. Yale University Press, 2008.

Hafner, Katie and Matthew Lyon. *Where Wizards Stay Up Late: The Origins of the Internet*. Simon & Schuster, 1998.

Hafstad, Vala. *Volcanic Eruption in the Air: Imminent Eruption*. CPI Books, 2018.

Head, Bessie. *A Question of Power*. 1973. Heinemann Educational Books, 2009.

Hemingway, Ernest. *A Moveable Feast*. 1964. Scribner, 1996.

Hesse, Herman. *The Return Home. Translated by Apostolos Stragalinos*. 1909. Greek edition. Kritiki Publicaitons, 2019.

Hoffman, Abbey. *Steal This Book*. 1971. Da Capo Press, 2002.

Hoffman, James. *The World Atlas of Coffee: From Beans to Brewing -- Coffees Explored, Explained and Enjoyed*. 2nd ed., Firefly Books, 2018.

Jasper, James M. *The Art of the Moral Protest: Culture, Biography, and Creativity in Social Movements*. 1997. University of Chicago Press, 1999.

Kenin, Alexandra. *Urban Trails: San Francisco: Coastal Bluffs/ The Presidio/ Hilltop Parks & Stairways*. Mountaineers Books, 2016.

Kotler, Steven and Jamie Wheal. *Stealing Fire: How Silicon Valley, the Navy SEALs, and Maverick Scientists Are Revolutionizing the Way We Live and Work*. Dey Street, 2018.

Lin-Chi. Zen *Teachings of Master Lin-Chi*. Translated by Burton Watson. Columbia University Press, 1999.

Machiavelli, Niccolo. *The Prince*. 1532. Translation by W. K. Marriott. Chartwell Books, 2008.

Mitchell, Jon. *In Real Life: Searching for Connection in High-Tech Times*. Parallax Press, 2014.

Moldvaer, Anette. *Coffee Obsession*. DK, 2014.

Niffenegger, Audrey. *The Time Traveler's Wife*. Harcourt, 2004.

Payne, Keith. *Broken Ladder: How Inequality Affects the Way We Think, Live, and Die*. Penguin Books, 2018.

Pilzer, Pozamoynt. *The Empty House*. Greek edition. Hodder and Stoughton Publications, 2013.

Prose, Francine, et al. *The Conde Nast Traveler Book of Unforgettable Journeys: Great Writers on Great Places*. Edited by Klara Glowczewska. Penguin Books, 2007.

Rahula, Walpola. *What the Buddha Taught*. 1959. 2nd ed., Grove Press, 1974.

Robinson, Richard, et al. *Buddhist Religions: A Historial Introduction*. 5th ed., Wadsworth, 2005.

Rongfu, Chen and PeiPei Yin. *Dharma Book for Busy People*. Chinese edition. Unknown publisher and date.

Safina, Carl. *Song for the Blue Ocean: Encounters Along the World's Coasts and Beneath the Seas*. Henry Holt & Co, 1998.

Schaller, George B. *The Serengeti Lion: A Study of Predator-Prey Relations*. University of Chicago Press, 1972.

Schmidt, Eric and Jonathan Rosenberg. *How Google Works*. Grand Central Publishing, 2017.

Schnakenberg, Robert. *Lost in Bill Murray*. Glenat, 2017.

Seitz, Matt Zoller. *The Wes Anderson Collection*. Abrams Books, 2013.

Shafak, Elif. *Three Daughters of Eve*. Georgian edition. Palette, 2016.

Shakespeare, William. *The Globe Illustrated Shakespeare: The Complete Works, Annotated*. 1979. Gramercy Books, 1998.

Sloan, Robin. *Sourdough: A Novel*. MCD, 2017.

Strauch, Barbara. *The Secret Life of the Grown-up Brain*. Penguin Books, 2011.

Strong, John S. *The Experience of Buddhism: Sources and Interpretations*. Wadsworth, 2001.

Suri, Manil. *The Death of Vishnu*. W.W. Norton & Company, 2001.

Suzuki, Shunryu. *Zen Mind, Beginner's Mind: Informal Talks on Zen Meditation and Practice*. 1970. Shambhala Publications, Inc., 2011.

Tegmark, Max. *Life 3.0: Being Human in the Age of Artificial Intelligence*. Vintage, 2018.

Umrigar, Thrity. *The Weight of Heaven: A Novel*. Harper, 2009.

Usigli, Rudolfo. *El Gesticulador: Pieza Para Demagogos En Tres Actos.* Pearson, 1974.

Virgil. *The Aeneid.* Translated by W. F. Jackson Knight. 1956. Penguin Books, 1958.

Wallace, Patricia. *The Psychology of the Internet.* Cambridge University Press, 1999.

West, Cornel. *Race Matters.* Vintage, 1993.

Yuson, Alfred A. *Philippines: Islands of Enchantment.* Photography by George Tapan. Tuttle Publishing, 2013.

www.ingramcontent.com/pod-product-compliance
Lightning Source LLC
Chambersburg PA
CBHW041422010526
44119CB00015B/345